ENGLISH

Curriculum Bank

KEY STAGE TWO
SCOTTISH LEVELS C-E

SPELLING AND PHONICS

ANNE WASHTELL AND LIZ LAYCOCK

Published by Scholastic Limited,
Villiers House,
Clarendon Avenue,
Leamington Spa,
Warwickshire CV32 5PR
Text © 1996 Anne Washtell and Liz Laycock
© 1996 Scholastic Limited

AUTHORS
ANNE WASHTELL AND LIZ LAYCOCK

EDITORS
CLARE GALLAHER
DEBORAH MARTIN

SERIES DESIGNER
LYNNE JOESBURY

DESIGNER
ANNA OLIWA

ILLUSTRATIONS
PAMELA VENUS

COVER ILLUSTRATION
JONATHAN BENTLEY

INFORMATION TECHNOLOGY CONSULTANT
MARTIN BLOWS

SCOTTISH 5–14 LINKS
MARGARET SCOTT AND SUSAN GOW

Designed using Aldus Pagemaker
Printed in Great Britain by Ebenezer Baylis, Worcester

British Library Cataloguing-in-Publication Data
A catalogue record for this book is available from the
British Library.

ISBN 0-590-53392-4

Contents

SPELLING AND
PHONICS KS2

ACKNOWLEDGEMENTS

The 'homophone handbook' idea was supplied by Carolyn Boyd, who found it a successful approach in her classroom because it helped the children to distinguish the meanings of words through graphic representation as well as by their spelling. The idea of making a topic-based dictionary was supplied by Alison Kelly.

The publishers gratefully acknowledge permission to reproduce the following copyright material:

Macmillan Children's Books for an extract from *Curtis the Hip-Hop Cat* by Gini Wade © Gini Wade (Macmillan Children's Books, 1986); Penguin Books Ltd for 'The Cat from Greece' from *My Cat Likes To Hide In Boxes* by Eve Sutton and Lynley Dodd © Eve Sutton and Lynley Dodd (Puffin, 1978); Scholastic Ltd for 'Down Behind The Dustbin' from *You Can't Catch Me* by Michael Rosen © Michael Rosen (Deutsch, 1981).

Every effort has been made to trace copyright holders for the works reproduced in this book, and the publishers apologise for any inadvertent admissions.

Introduction

Scholastic Curriculum Bank is a series for all primary teachers, providing an essential planning tool for devising comprehensive schemes of work as well as an easily accessible and varied bank of practical, classroom-tested activities with photocopiable resources.

Designed to help planning for and implementation of progression, differentiation and assessment, *Scholastic Curriculum Bank* offers a structured range of stimulating activities with clearly-stated learning objectives that reflect the programmes of study, and detailed lesson plans that allow busy teachers to put ideas into practice with the minimum amount of preparation time. The photocopiable sheets that accompany many of the activities provide ways of integrating purposeful application of knowledge and skills, differentiation, assessment and record-keeping.

Opportunities for assessment are highlighted within the activities where appropriate. Ways of using information technology for different purposes and in different contexts, as a tool for communicating and handling information and as a means of investigating, are integrated into the activities where appropriate, and more explicit guidance is provided at the end of the book.

The series covers all the primary curriculum subjects, with separate books for Key Stages 1 and 2 or Scottish Levels A–B and C–E. It can be used as a flexible resource with any scheme, to fulfil National Curriculum and Scottish 5–14 requirements and to provide children with a variety of different learning experiences that will lead to effective acquisition of skills and knowledge.

SCHOLASTIC CURRICULUM BANK ENGLISH

The *Scholastic Curriculum Bank English* books enable teachers to plan comprehensive and structured coverage of the English curriculum, and enable pupils to develop the required skills, knowledge and understanding through activities.

Each book covers one key stage. There are four books for Key Stage 1/Scottish levels A–B and four for Key Stage 2/Scottish levels C–E. These books reflect the English programme of study, so that there are titles on Reading, Writing, Speaking and listening and Spelling and phonics.

Bank of activities

This book provides a bank of activities that provide opportunities to talk about similarities and differences in words, as well as opportunities to play with words and take part in word games. Such contexts capitalise on children's interest in language and provide valuable learning areas.

Lesson plans

Detailed lesson plans, under clear headings, are given for each activity and provide material for immediate implementation in the classroom. The structure for each activity is as follows:

Activity title box

The information contained in the box at the beginning of each activity outlines the following key aspects:
▲ *Activity title and learning objective*. For each activity a clearly stated learning objective is given in bold italics. These learning objectives break down aspects of the programmes of study into manageable, hierarchical teaching and learning chunks, and their purpose is to aid planning for progression. These objectives can easily be referenced to the National Curriculum and Scottish 5–14 requirements by using the overview grids at the end of this chapter (pages 9 to 12).
▲ *Class organisation/Likely duration*. Icons †† and ⏲ signpost the suggested group sizes for each activity and the approximate amount of time required to complete it.

Previous skills/knowledge needed

Information is given here when it is necessary for the children to have acquired specific knowledge or skills prior to carrying out the activity.

Key background information

The information in this section outlines the areas of study covered by each activity and gives a general background to the particular topic or theme, outlining the basic skills that will be developed and the ways in which the activity will address children's learning.

Preparation

Advice is given for those occasions where it is necessary for the teacher to prime the pupils for the activity or to prepare materials, or to set up a display or activity ahead of time.

Resources needed

All of the materials needed to carry out the activity are listed, so that the pupils or the teacher can gather them together easily before the beginning of the teaching session.

What to do

Easy-to-follow, step-by-step instructions are given for carrying out the activity, including (where appropriate) suggested questions for the teacher to ask the pupils to help instigate discussion and stimulate investigation.

Suggestion(s) for extension/support

Ideas are given for ways of providing easy differentiation where activities lend themselves to this purpose. In all cases, suggestions are provided as to ways in which each activity can be modified for less able or extended for more able children.

Assessment opportunities

Where appropriate, opportunities for ongoing teacher assessment of the children's work during or after a specific activity are highlighted.

Opportunities for IT

Where opportunities for IT present themselves, these are briefly outlined with reference to particularly suitable types of program. The chart on page 158 presents specific areas of IT covered in the activities, together with more detailed support on how to apply particular types of program. Selected lesson plans serve as models for other activities by providing more comprehensive guidance on the application of IT, and these are indicated by the bold page numbers on the grid and the 💻 icon at the start of an activity.

Display ideas

Where they are relevant and innovative, display ideas are incorporated into activity plans and illustrated with examples.

Aspects of the English PoS covered

Inevitably, as all areas of English are interrelated, activities will cover aspects of the programmes of study in other areas of the English curriculum. These links are highlighted under this heading.

Reference to photocopiable sheets

Where activities include photocopiable sheets, small reproductions of these are included in the lesson plans together with guidance notes for their use and, where appropriate, suggested answers.

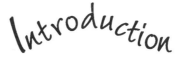

Assessment

Children's development as spellers will take place over time. For this reason we have included photocopiable record sheets for different aspects of phonics and spelling knowledge, rather than suggesting one-off summative assessments. Activities which refer to an assessment sheet are indicated by the ✍ icon. However, every activity provides an opportunity for teachers to observe and record aspects of individual children's development knowledge, skill and understanding of words, letters, alphabetical order, spelling patterns, use of dictionaries and so on. It is suggested that a copy of each record sheet is made for each child and that a file is created for these. At the end of a school year, if they are completed regularly, they will give a great deal of detailed information about each child's spelling ability. Some activity sheets (for example, in the activity 'What do you know about the alphabet?') could be used as diagnostic, baseline assessments of children's current knowledge, and these too should be added to the child's file. Diagnostic activities will contribute to teachers' understanding of a child's spelling and enable plans to be made to offer appropriate support and teaching.

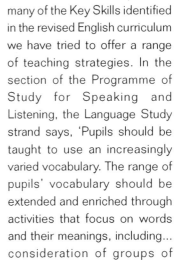

Photocopiable activity sheets

Many of the activities are accompanied by photocopiable activity sheets. For some activities, there may be more than one version to provide differentiation by task. Other sheets may be more open-ended to provide differentiation by outcome. The photocopiable activity sheets provide purposeful activities that are ideal for assessment and can be kept as records in pupils' portfolios of work.

Cross-curricular links

Cross-curricular links are identified on a simple grid which cross-references the particular areas of study in English to the programmes of study for other subjects in the curriculum, and where appropriate provides suggestions for activities (see page 160).

SPELLING AND PHONICS

In compiling this set of activities, we have not set out to offer a prescribed order for teaching different aspects of spelling and phonics but we have tried to offer activities which draw on children's existing knowledge and attempt to take this further. Some activities will be appropriate for children who are at an early stage in their understanding of both phonics and spelling, while others will require quite high levels of knowledge and understanding. The activites can be adapted for children who require greater challenge or for those who might have difficulties (see 'Suggestions for extension/ support' on opposite page).

The National Curriculum Programme of Study for English at Key Stage 2 (1995) has influenced the areas that we have chosen to focus upon. For many of the Key Skills identified in the revised English curriculum we have tried to offer a range of teaching strategies. In the section of the Programme of Study for Speaking and Listening, the Language Study strand says, 'Pupils should be taught to use an increasingly varied vocabulary. The range of pupils' vocabulary should be extended and enriched through activities that focus on words and their meanings, including... consideration of groups of words, for example word families, the range of words relevant to a topic.' An important element in all of these activities is the generation of interest in and enthusiasm for language, its history and its forms.

There is also a requirement in the Writing section of the Programme of Study to focus on Language Study, which at Key Stage 2 stipulates that 'pupils should be taught to distinguish between words of similar meaning, to explain the meanings of words and to experiment with choices of vocabulary. Their interest in words should be extended by the discussion of language use and choices.' We have attempted to develop a genuine 'interest in words' because we believe that such an interest sustains children's efforts to manipulate and use language accurately. Some of the activities, therefore, look into the roots and history of words, as well as offering contexts for learning about their spelling.

Inevitably, at Key Stage 2, the focus of a book like this will shift from phonics to a deeper consideration of spelling because it is at this stage that great strides will be made in the development of conventional spelling. It is perhaps worth reviewing what we currently understand about children's spelling development. Since 1981, when Gentry published his analysis of the stages children appear to move through in their development as spellers ('Learning to Spell Developmentally', *Reading Teacher*, 34/4), we have been able to understand much more of the processes involved. This research suggests that there are five main stages in the development of a child's spelling.

SPELLING AND PHONICS KS2

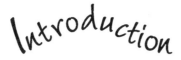

Pre-communicative

At this stage the child knows that letters, sometimes numbers, and letter-like shapes are intended to communicate meaning. The child does not have any idea of letter/sound correspondence, so letters are strung randomly together to represent the child's current concept of what writing is.

Semi-phonetic

At this stage the child demonstrates some knowledge of the alphabetic nature of writing and some phonic knowledge, though she will often use the 'letter-name strategy' to represent the sounds of words: for example, 'R' will stand for 'are'. The child often uses one or two letters to represent a whole word, but has a growing understanding of the left to right order of letters and a growing knowledge of the alphabet.

Phonetic

By now the child realises that the sounds in words can be represented by letters and usually works hard to represent each sound she can hear. Letters are used entirely on the basis of the child's understanding of their sounds, with little regard for conventional letter sequences. At this stage children are often enthusiastic writers and it is essential to approach 'correction' with care, because confidence evaporates very quickly. It is at this point that many spellers get stuck, so it is important, too, to move them on to *looking* at words, as well as hearing them.

Transitional

The child has realised that words and syllables contain vowels and begins to pay attention to orthographic principles. She is beginning to develop some visual strategies for spelling and this will often lead to the correct letters appearing in the wrong order, for example 'huose' for 'house'. It is now that the transition from dependence on the sounds of words to greater use of visual strategies and visual information in words takes place. Direct teaching about spelling and focusing on the letter strings and patterns in words is particularly beneficial during this stage.

Correct

The child now consistently spells the majority of words in a growing vocabulary correctly, or very nearly correctly. She uses silent letters correctly, knows the spelling of homonyms, contractions and polysyllabic words and uses mainly visual strategies to learn the spelling of new words – she will often

say, 'That doesn't *look* right.'

Although we can now identify each of these stages in children's spelling, we still cannot be absolutely certain that any one teaching method or approach will enable all children to become good spellers. What does seem to be clear, from this research as well as from that of Margaret Peters (*Spelling: Caught or Taught? – A New Look,* Routledge, 1990) is that children need to be helped to move away from drawing exclusively on their awareness of sounds in words and encouraged to draw on internalised visual patterns within words. To this end, a very practical strategy for learning words has been proposed – the 'look–cover–write–check' routine. This learning strategy was recommended in the earlier version of the National Curriculum's Non-statutory Guidance (1988) and is taken from Margaret Peters' work.

How to learn a new word:

LOOK at the word carefully and in such a way that you will remember what you have seen.

COVER the word so that you cannot see it.

WRITE the word from memory, saying it softly to yourself as you are writing.

CHECK what you have written. If you have not written the word correctly, do not alter it, instead go back and repeat all these steps again. (Margaret Peters, 1985)

Activities like Kim's Game and Pelmanism, which are described in this book, are useful ways of developing the skills of looking and remembering. Some words will also be remembered through an understanding of how the language works and through a knowledge of some of the rules that govern it. There are problems sometimes with learning rules because there are often exceptions. Where a rule has a fairly consistent application, we have used it to guide and remind children of particular spellings.

English spelling often appears to be illogical, but it makes more sense once one knows why certain things happen. Many of the reasons for strange spellings lie in the history of the language and the way English has absorbed vocabulary from the many influences of its past. The study of the history of English appeals strongly to children, who like solving mysteries, so this is a strong thread running through many of the activities. Information which might be a useful point of reference for teachers is included in the Appendix (pages 91 to 93). The final chapter includes some of the many curious things about written English. We hope that teachers will use these as starting points for developing ideas to find out about and investigate the curiosities of English.

Overview grid

Learning objective	PoS/AO	Content	Type of activity	Page
Alphabetic and dictionary knowledge				
To provide children with further experience of learning the alphabet and thinking about its sequence.	Sp. & List.: 1a. Reading: 1b. Writing KS1: 2d; KS2: 2d, e; 3c. *Reading for Information: Level B.*	Reviewing knowledge of the alphabet and looking at the position of letters in relation to others.	Whole class discussion. Quiz in pairs, then individual activity using photocopied sheets.	14
To help children recognise and reflect on their increasing power to spell words correctly.	Sp. & List.: 1a. Reading: 1b. Writing: 2d. *Spelling: Level B.*	Independent unaided spelling of all the words the child knows.	Individual activity, done as whole class, listing words.	16
To enable pupils to utilise their alphabetic knowledge in order to organise and refer back to a bank of words that they can spell correctly.	Writing: 2b, d, e. *Spelling: Level B. Reading for Information: Level B.*	Organising a list of known words on to an alphabet sheet and then into dictionaries.	Individual activity, sorting words alphabetically.	18
To equip children with essential terminology to enable them to talk analytically about words.	Sp. & List.: 2a. Writing: 2d. *Knowledge about Language: Level B.*	Introducing terms 'vowel' and 'consonant'. Completing quiz.	Whole class introduction, then individual activity using differentiated quiz sheets.	20
To raise children's awareness that vowels can be long or short and to enable them to talk about this.	Sp. & List.: 2a. Writing: 2d. *Spelling: Level B.*	Using pictures/objects to differentiate between words with long and short vowels.	Whole class introduction. Individual completion of activity sheet.	22
To enable children to construct a simple dictionary.	Sp. & List.: 1a. Reading: 1b, 2c. Writing: 2d. *Spelling: Level B.*	Using class word bank as the basis for making a dictionary. Making use of initial and subsequent letters of words.	Working in pairs to organise a list of words and then to sort them before putting in a dictionary.	25
To enable children to locate efficiently initial letters in the dictionary.	Sp. & List.: 1a. Reading: 1b. Writing: 2d. *Reading for Information: Level B.*	Using alphabet cards, children should locate letters in the dictionary, as rapidly as possible.	Two pairs of children, working as teams.	29
To enable children to find common words in the dictionary.	Sp. & List.: 1c. Reading: 2c. Writing: 2d. *Reading for Information: Level B.*	Using word cards to find words as quickly as possible; self-evaluation of progress.	Two pairs, in teams, challenging each other to locate words. Completion of self-evaluation sheet.	31
To enable children to understand the purpose of headwords in dictionaries and how to use them.	Sp. & List.: 2a. Reading: 1b. Writing: 2d. *Reading for Information: Level B.*	Using word cards to find headwords as quickly as possible.	Two pairs in teams, using question cards. Individual record sheet completion.	34

SPELLING AND PHONICS KS2

Learning objective	PoS/AO	Content	Type of activity	Page
To create a way of recording information about spelling and making a reference resource relevant to the individual child. To introduce terminology about spelling and words.	Writing 2d. *Spelling: Level B.*	Making booklet with alphabetical section, rules, ways of remembering spellings. Making contents page.	Whole class initial explanation. Working individually to make up booklets, then using booklets as/when appropriate thereafter.	37
Rhymes and homophones				
To enable children to develop an interest in homophones and use them in their writing.	Sp. & List.: 1a, c. Reading: 2a, c. Writing: 2b, d. *Knowledge about Language: Level B.*	Introductory session and use of term 'homophone'. Writing short individual homophone stories.	Whole class discussion about homophones, using prepared list. Individual story writing (brainstorm/draft/discuss/write).	40
To provide children with experience of listening to rhyme and alliteration and to relate the sound patterns that they hear to the patterns of letters in print.	Sp. & List.: 1a. Reading: 1a, 2a. Writing: 1c, 2d. *Knowledge about Language: Level B. Spelling: Level B.*	Reading aloud rhyming poems; revising understanding of rhyme. Looking at different spellings of same sound and at where alliteration is in a particular poem.	Whole class discussion about rhyme/alliteration/spelling of homophones. Learning poem by heart.	42
To develop children's understanding of homophones.	Sp. & List. 1a. Reading: 2a, c. Writing: 2d. *Spelling: Level B.*	Reading aloud a rhyming poem, identifying rhymes/ rhyme families/meanings of homophones. Identifying and illustrating homophone pairs, to show meanings. Using term 'homophone'.	Whole class introduction to rhyming poem. Individual contributions to class book.	44
To help children recognise that there are alternative ways of spelling the same sound and to analyse what some of these alternatives might be through the use of appropriate terminology. To introduce the term 'homophone'.	Reading: 2a. Writing: 2a, d, e. *Spelling: Level B.*	Identifying rhymes in a poem, then listing other words which rhyme; identifying homophones and different letter clusters creating the same sound and letter families.	Whole class or group, then pairs/individuals. Introduction through rhyming poems, then worksheets on rhymes and homophones.	47
To focus on rhymes and the different spellings of homophones.	Sp. & List.: 1a. Reading: 2a. Writing: 2d. *Spelling: Level B. Imaginative Writing: Level B.*	Sharing rhyming poems. Identifying rhyme pattern. Children writing own verses keeping same pattern. Reviewing and identifying spelling patterns.	Whole class, then groups/ pairs. Opportunities for discussion of rhymes, spelling, homophones, half-rhymes and to focus on particular spelling patterns children need to learn.	50
To raise children's awareness that there are alternative ways of spelling the same sound. To develop this awareness through discussion and oral presentation.	Sp. & List: 1a. Reading: 2a. Writing: 2a, d, e. *Spelling: Level B. Imaginative Writing: Level C.*	Introduction to limerick form and rhyme pattern. Collecting sets of rhymes. Children composing limericks, then sharing verses and analysing differences in spelling.	Whole class working as individuals, then pairs. Discussion and oral presentation.	52

SPELLING AND PHONICS KS2

Learning objective	PoS/AO	Content	Type of activity	Page
To use children's love of jokes and puns to look at words which sound the same, but have different meanings or spellings (homophones).	Writing: 2d. *Imaginative Writing: Level C.*	Collecting and sharing jokes which play on words, especially those which use homophones. Making class joke book.	Whole class introduction, then several periods of time working as groups/ individuals, writing out jokes.	55
Chapter 3 – Word families				
To enable children to identify constant letter strings in words.	Reading: 2a. Writing: 2d. *Spelling: Level B.*	Using letter strings in children's own names to start collections of words with the same strings.	Whole class, then individual activity.	58
To introduce the term 'prefix'. To focus on the meanings of the common prefixes 'mis-' and 'dis-'.	Sp. & List.: 3b. Reading: 2a. Writing: 2d. *Spelling: Level D.*	Explanation of the role of the prefix and the meaning of 'mis-' and 'dis-' (negative prefixes). Adding prefixes to root words (cards and worksheet); checking spelling.	Whole class/group explanation, then children working in pairs.	59
To enable children to understand the meanings of common prefixes.	Writing: 2d. *Spelling: Level D.*	Card game, matching prefixes with their meanings.	Large group for explanation, then pairs playing Pelmanism-style game.	61
To familiarise children with the meaning and use of common prefixes.	Sp. & List.: 3b. Reading: 2a. Writing: 2d. *Spelling: Level D.*	Using prefixes derived from Latin and Greek; locating words using these and finding out meanings. Filling in prefix webs.	Short introduction with whole group, then pairs or small groups.	62
To familiarise children with the meaning, use and spelling of the suffixes '-ful', '-fully', '-ness', '-less'.	Reading: 2a. Writing: 2d. *Spelling: Level D.*	Applying rules about the spelling of words with common suffixes.	Individuals learning rules about addition of suffixes – completing activity sheet.	65
To encourage 'looking with intent'. To learn the vowel digraphs 'oe', 'ui', 'ue', 'ie'.	Reading: 2a. Writing: 2d. *Spelling: Level B.*	Timed memorising of spelling of words with common vowel digraphs. Kim's Game to promote 'looking with intent'.	Small groups or pairs.	66
To demonstrate something of the complex history of the English language and to stimulate interest in investigating word roots and origins.	Sp. & List.: 3b. Reading: 2a. Writing: 2d, 3. *Spelling: Level D.*	Starting a long-term investigation of the history of English and roots of words, to demonstrate language change and growth.	Whole class introduction, then ongoing activity over a period of time for groups or individuals.	68
Chapter 4 – Curiosities				
To focus attention on words which have a double consonant. To encourage 'looking with intent' at letter patterns in words.	Reading: 2a. Writing: 2d. *Spelling: Level C.*	Identifying words in wordsearch grid of words spelled with double consonants.	Individual activity, completing wordsearch sheet.	72

Learning objective	PoS/AO	Content	Type of activity	Page
To familiarise children with the plural endings of nouns ending in 'y' ('s' or 'ies').	Reading: 2a. Writing: 2d. *Spelling: Level C.*	Identifying which words add 's' and which 'ies' in the plural, through application of the rule.	Individual/pairs card game, adding plural endings to words.	73
To reinforce children's knowledge of the shortened forms of words, using apostrophes.	Sp. & List.: 3b Reading: 2a. Writing: 2c, d. *Knowledge about Language: Level E.*	Contractions of words to be matched with full forms of words in lotto game.	Groups of five or seven children, one of whom will be a caller.	74
To enable children to recognise and understand the funtion of the silent 'k'.	Sp. & List.: 1a, 3b. Writing: 2d. *Spelling: Level C.*	Playing board game which requires the identifying of the spelling of words with a silent 'k'.	Short introduction. Main activity playing the game in small groups (even numbers), then short follow-up.	76
To investigate inconsistent spelling patterns. To familiarise children with 'gh' and 'wh' spelling patterns.	Sp. & List.: 3b. Writing: 2d. *Spelling: Level C.*	Story-based activity requiring correction of words which have 'h' missed out, and learning of the reason for curious spellings.	Intended for competent readers and writers. Large group for introduction, then paired or individual activity.	78
To raise children's awareness that consonants can be hard or soft and to enable them to talk about this.	Sp. & List.: 2a. Reading: 2a. Writing: 2d. *Spelling: Level B. Knowledge about Language: Level D.*	Using terminology 'vowel' and 'consonant'. Focusing on letter 'c' and when the pronunciation is hard/soft.	Whole group followed by work in pairs or individually. Completing written activity.	80
To help children recognise and understand the function of silent 'b'.	Sp. & List.: 1a; 3b. Reading: 2b. Writing: 2b; 3c. *Spelling: Level C.*	Explanation of silent 'b' in spelling. Completion of silent 'b' crossword. Differentiated versions.	Whole class introduction, then individual/paired work.	83
To enable children to recognise and understand the function of silent 'e'.	Writing: 2d, e; 3c. *Spelling: Level B. Knowledge about Language: Level D.*	Using terminology 'vowel'/ 'consonant'. Categorising words with silent 'e' with both long and short vowel sounds. Writing and presenting information about words under different headings.	Best undertaken over two sessions. Whole group introduction, then pair work. Writing up information and preparation of display.	85
To help children become familiar with more irregular phonic patterns.	Sp. & List.: 3b. Reading: 2a, b. Writing: 2b. *Spelling: Level D.*	Focus on 'sc' consonant blend. Completion of crossword using word bank of 'sc' words for reference.	Whole group, then individual/paired activity.	89

Entries given in italics relate to the Scottish English Language 5–14 National guidelines.

SPELLING AND PHONICS KS2

Alphabetic & dictionary knowledge

The Programmes of Study in Key Stage 2 place strong emphasis on the application of alphabetic knowledge. Children are required to 'read and use a wide range of sources of information, including reference materials, encyclopaedias and dictionaries'.

When children use a dictionary, not only do they need a thorough knowledge of the alphabetic sequence, but they have to be able to manipulate it effectively; they can no longer solely rely on knowing the initial letter when looking for words but they have to be able to utilise the subsequent letters.

The role of devices such as headwords in dictionaries has to be learned but, for these to be useful, children need to be able to apply their alphabetic knowledge very rapidly and to be able to calculate whether the word they are seeking falls alphabetically between the two headwords on the page (or double-page spread). This is a challenging task and on the child's part takes confident knowledge of the position of letters in relation to others.

The activities in this chapter aim to provide practice and experience in all these areas. There is some overlap with Key Stage 1 to enable teachers to check existing alphabetic knowledge so that gaps and areas of need can be identified. Other activities emphasise the various skills that children need to acquire in order to manipulate dictionaries and encyclopaedias. There is also a focus on looking more closely at vowels and consonants and their role in words. These activities are intended to provide children with knowledge and essential terminology that will help them as they work with other activities in the book.

WHAT DO YOU KNOW ABOUT THE ALPHABET?

To provide children with further experience of learning the alphabet and thinking about its sequence.

†† *Whole class and then individuals.*

🕐 *40 minutes.*

Previous skills/knowledge needed

Children will need to have had experience of reciting and writing the alphabet. They may still lack confidence in some areas of knowledge, for example continuing the alphabet from different points in the sequence. They may know how some letters are positioned in relation to others but this knowledge may be incomplete.

Key background information

At Key Stage 2 Levels C–E children are expected to apply their knowledge of the alphabet and its sequence. They have to be able to manipulate not only initial letters of words but also subsequent letters in the alphabetic sequence. This knowledge is vital if they are to be able to retrieve information from a wide range of reference sources including dictionaries and encyclopaedias. Therefore it is essential that they feel confident and secure in their alphabetic knowledge. This activity sets out to brush up this knowledge and will enable teachers to identify gaps.

Preparation

On the first page of the flip chart, write the alphabet. On the second page write the sentence 'The quick brown fox jumps over the lazy dog'. Make copies of photocopiable pages 96 and 97, one of each per child. Prepare alphabet strips (that is, strips of paper with the letters of the alphabet written in sequence) for those children who need them.

Resources needed

Flip chart or chalkboard, photocopiable sheets 96 and 97, pens, pencils, alphabet strips, alphabet books, dictionaries, rough paper, blank cards, an encyclopaedia, card index box, a set of cards and 'dividers'.

What to do

Explain to the children that the aim of the session is to remind themselves how much they already know about the alphabet. Start off with a brief piece of language study. Explain to the children the derivation of the word *alphabet*. (It comes from the Greek language, with *alpha* being the name of the first letter of the Greek alphabet and *beta* being the name of the second.) Ask the children what *alpha* and *beta* might be called in English.

Next, distribute the rough paper for the children to work on in pairs (or individually, if preferred). Explain that they will need the paper to jot down notes during a brief, five-minute alphabet quiz. Introduce the quiz by explaining that the intention is for the group to establish some facts about the alphabet. Ask the children the following questions:

▲ Can you write the complete alphabet? If so, write the letters down in the correct order.

▲ How many letters are there in the alphabet?

▲ Which letters are the vowels? Write them down.

▲ How many vowels are there in the alphabet?

Once the children have completed the quiz, ask them to report back on the facts. Collate these on the flip chart or chalkboard. The facts that will have been established will include: the correct written sequence of the alphabet; the total number of letters in the alphabet; the number of

consonants; the number of vowels and the names of the vowels.

Move on now to focus on the sequence of the alphabet. Turn the page of the flip chart to show the famous sentence 'The quick brown fox jumps over the lazy dog'. With the whole group helping, point out that the full alphabet is represented in the sentence. Point to all the letters and name them. Then, at random, select different letters of the alphabet, write them on the flip chart and ask the children to work in pairs and as quickly as possible to write the letter that comes before and the letter that comes after each one. Collate the answers on the chart. The children have now rehearsed the key areas for the differentiated worksheets (pages 96 and 97). These should be undertaken independently and will take approximately 15 minutes. Allow 10 minutes at the end of the session to review the content of the worksheets with the whole group. Check that all children can recite and write the alphabet in sequence and that they can identify the vowels. Attention should be paid to letters that come 'before' and 'after'.

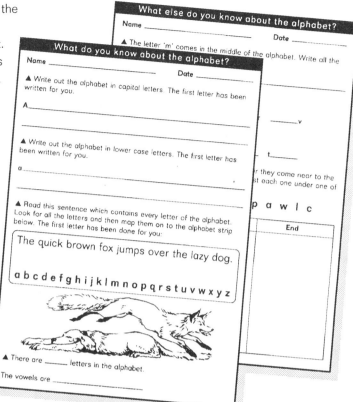

Suggestion(s) for extension

Children who show confidence in handling the alphabet can compile a set of 'encyclopaedia quiz cards' for the other children to use. These should focus particularly on applying their knowledge of working with the alphabetic sequence from different points. They should work with a class encyclopaedia or large reference book. The quiz cards could contain such questions as: 'If you want to find "dinosaurs" should you look before cats or after cats?' 'Does the dogs page come before the Egypt page or after it?' These cards should be accompanied by a set of answer cards. (This could be further developed as a main activity for those who require more support.)

Suggestion(s) for support

This support activity is suitable for children who are still revealing weaknesses in their alphabetic knowledge. Provide these children with an alphabet strip (they could be given a blank strip to fill in first of all), a card index box and a set of cards and ask them to compile a card index in alphabetical order of every child's name in the class. Establish with the children a useful future purpose for the card index (for example, to contain dated entries on books that the children would recommend others to read). The group should write each child's name on an individual card. (The teacher's discretion is needed as to whether to work only with forenames or to set the index up by surnames.) Ask the group to sort the names into alphabetical order, with the name which is nearest to the start of the alphabet at the front of the box. They should refer back to the alphabet strip if they are unsure about the order. They could also make 'divider' cards of the complete alphabet and slot these in appropriately

among the name cards. The children may need support if they are dealing with two names that start with the same letter.

Assessment opportunities

The alphabet quiz at the start of the main activity could be undertaken individually and form a baseline assessment on the children's alphabetic knowledge. The results of the children's participation in the whole class activity and in their individual work on the worksheets should indicate clearly those who have a sound knowledge of the alphabet and its sequence and those who will need more practice.

The extension activity provides a context for thinking about the position of letters in relation to other letters, which is an important skill that children need to develop if they are to use dictionaries and encyclopaedias efficiently. Assessments should be based on how other children work with the cards and how effectively they use the encyclopaedia to help them reach their answers.

The support activity will not only help those children who are still unsure of the order of the alphabet but also make demands on their existing knowledge. Note which letters the children are confident with and where confusion and uncertainties lie. The children may need to refer to the alphabet books or alphabet strips to help them.

Display ideas

Display the 'encyclopaedia quiz' cards and provide blank answer sheets for the children to write on. Explain to the

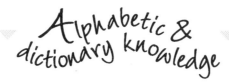

children the ground rules for the answer cards. The card index will require a purpose that suits the needs of the class. This should then be regularly used by all the children. The cards should be 'muddled' so that those children who need the practice could be asked to sort them out again.

Aspects of the English PoS covered

Speaking and listening – 1a.
Reading – 1b.
Writing KS1 – 2d; KS2 – 2d, e; 3c.

Reference to photocopiable sheets

After practising on rough paper by answering the questions referred to in the main activity, the children can each fill in photocopiable page 96 and then photocopiable page 97.

ALL THE WORDS I CAN SPELL

To help children recognise and reflect on their increasing power to spell words correctly.

†† *Individuals. (You could use this activity with the whole class or with small groups of children who need practice in spelling.)*

🕒 *A minimum of 20–40 minutes.*

Previous skills/knowledge needed

Children will need to show some evidence of being able to spell a number of words correctly. For example, in their independent writing, they will increasingly reveal a bank of words which they can spell correctly. They will be able to identify these words as being correctly spelled and may be able to identify other words that have errors in them.

Key background information

Glenda Bissex's famous case study of her son Paul (*Gnys at Wrk: A Child Learns to Write and Read*, Harvard University Press, 1985) demonstrated that children go through identifiable stages of development in learning to spell. Her research was developed by Gentry who ascribed names to the stages, starting with precommunicative through to correct spelling ('Learning to Spell Developmentally', *Reading Teacher*, 34/4). This research has provided teachers with valuable insights when

looking at spelling errors and has led to children being encouraged to 'have a go' at spelling words for themselves. This approach needs balancing, however, by helping children to recognise that words are spelled in conventional ways and that this is ultimately what they are aiming for. The purpose, therefore, of this activity is to help children identify their existing bank of words that they can spell correctly. The activity should provide teachers with an opportunity to gather evidence for formative assessment purposes at different points in the year. If possible, this lesson should be followed up with the next activity to form a second session.

Preparation

Write on the flip chart or chalkboard the heading 'All the words that I can spell'. Provide enough A4 paper and writing materials for each child.

Resources needed

Sheets of A4 paper (enough for one sheet for each child), pens, pencils, flip chart or chalkboard, sticky tape or masking tape.

What to do

Explain to the children that they will be making a long list of words. It will be called 'All the words I can spell'. Draw their attention to the heading written on the flip chart. They should try to list only words that they think they can spell correctly. The list can include words that they have used in their writing and words they have read. Explain that they will work on the list for about 15 minutes. Field any queries – such as 'Can we use dictionaries?' or 'Can I include the name of my favourite pop group?' – and then give out the A4 paper and

writing materials. After five minutes, visit any children who have not made a strong start and provide them with support (see 'Suggestion(s) for support').

Once the children have exhausted their list, look at it with them and ask them to check for any words that they may not have spelled quite correctly (these could be carefully underlined or circled in pencil by the child). If they have made errors then see if they can correct them, perhaps by using a 'have a go' technique. 'Have a go' usually means writing the word down in three different ways to see if the spelling can be sorted out. Help the child identify any other words that are not yet ready to be included in the final list. To conclude the session, ask the children to pair up and read their lists out to their neighbours.

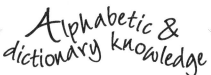

Suggestion(s) for extension

Children who are able should try to correct any errors in their list. They could then be given another sheet of A4 paper on which they can list 'All the words I can nearly spell'. The children should pick several of these words to try to correct themselves. If they succeed, these can be added to their main list. They could then take a few more words and refer to a dictionary to try to locate the correct spelling. If they succeed, they should practise writing the correctly spelled word using the 'look cover write check' technique (see page 8).

Children who clearly enjoyed the activity and successfully compiled their list can move on to the next activity, 'Making a personal dictionary'.

Suggestion(s) for support

Some children will reveal difficulties at a very early stage in this activity. Help these children to discover how much they know by carefully opening up their options. Suggest to them that they can put names on their lists: they may be able to spell the names of some of their friends, of brothers, sisters, pets and favourite food and drink. They may well be able to spell words that are linked to a particular interest or hobby. Encourage them to write down all the little words they know, such as 'yes' and 'no'. In discussion ask the children to suggest words that they think they can almost spell. Ask them to write some of these down and discuss them together.

Assessment opportunities

The number of correctly spelled words will be an obvious indicator of a child's growing bank of known words. The child's ability to review his list and identify words that have been incorrectly spelled should also be noted. The success of self-correction strategies, such as 'have a go', should be noted. If this activity is carried out at key points in the school year, a clear picture of the child's progress can be made. If previous lists have been retained, these can be used in future discussions with the child for comparative purposes in order to promote the child's ability to monitor and evaluate his own progress.

Opportunities for IT

The children could use a word processor to make a class list of 'All the words I can spell' for display purposes in the classroom. The list could be saved on a disk and added to, being reprinted at various times. Children could also be shown how to use the spelling checker facility of their word processor to check that all the spellings are correct and that there have been no typing mistakes as the list was entered.

Once all the words have been entered, children can experiment with suitable fonts, sizes and formatting commands to make the list attractive for display in the classroom.

Display ideas

These lists are primarily individual, but a blank chart labelled 'All the words we can spell in the whole world' could be displayed on the wall and all the children encouraged to add known words to the class list.

Aspects of the English PoS covered

Speaking and listening – 1a.
Reading – 1b.
Writing – 2d.

MAKING A PERSONAL DICTIONARY

To enable pupils to utilise their alphabetic knowledge in order to organise and refer back to a bank of words that they can spell correctly.

✝✝ *Whole class or groups, working as individuals.*

🕐 *30 minutes–1 hour.*

Previous skills/knowledge needed

Children will have a bank of known words and will have written an extensive list of all the words that they know (see previous activity). They will have used a range of strategies to check that their list of words is spelled correctly. They will have had experience of sorting a bank of words into alphabetical order.

Key background information

See 'Key background information' for the previous activity, 'All the words I can spell'. In order to raise children's awareness of their growing knowledge of correctly spelled words, it is useful if these are organised into a personal dictionary and children then encouraged to use it. Children tend to make spelling errors that fall into the category of 'careless mistakes'. This implies that they really know the spelling, but may be hurrying in order to focus on what they are trying to say. By encouraging them to proofread their work they can use their personal dictionary to double-check on these errors. If children are taught to use a personal dictionary in this way, they are less likely to queue up to ask for every word that they think they need.

The dictionaries compiled in this activity are intended for this special bank of known words and preferably should not be used on subsequent occasions as a general 'wordbook' for unknown spellings (although as the child accumulates more known spellings these could be added). Every teacher has experienced the frustration of a child asking for a word that is already in his book. This can occur either because the child has not been trained to look first to see if the word is there or because he simply cannot read the word. A personal dictionary should provide children with a more constructive and successful approach in the early days of using a dictionary.

Preparation

Either use small blank notebooks or make special books (see 'Resources' and 'Preparation' sections on in the activity 'From word bank to dictionary' on page 25). You will need one for each child. Prepare enough alphabet strips to have one on each table. Photocopy the support sheet (photocopiable page 98) for rough working, one for each child who might need it. Write the heading 'All the words I can spell' on the flip chart.

Resources needed

Blank notebooks (one for each child), child's list of 'All the words I can spell', pens, pencils, alphabet strips, flip chart, photocopiable sheets 98 and 99, six small counters of different colours, a set of thin felt-tipped pens of matching colours, dictionaries.

What to do

If this does not follow immediately on from the previous activity, remind the children of the lists they compiled of all the words that they could spell correctly. Explain that in this activity they will be making personal dictionaries entitled 'All the words I can spell'. Show the children the blank books and explain that the purpose of making the dictionaries is to help them organise their list of words so that if they need to check any spellings when they are writing, they can do this quickly and efficiently. Ask the children how a dictionary works. Collect their ideas. You should be looking for knowledge about the alphabetic organisation and about the ordering of words within each alphabetic section. Tell the children that first they must write the title and their name on the front of the dictionary and then label each page of the book in sequence with a letter of the alphabet. Give the books out and allow ten minutes for everyone to prepare their dictionaries. Direct those children who need support to the alphabet strips.

After this, stop the whole group for a few moments and explain that the next step will be to take their list of 'All the words I can spell' and begin to organise the words alphabetically. They should then write them into the dictionaries. (At this point, some children should be directed to the photocopiable alphabet sheets – see 'Suggestion(s)

All the words I can spell: alphabet sheet

Name _____ Date _____

▲ Use this sheet *first* before you write your list of words into your dictionary. You need your 'All the words I can spell' list. Look at the first letter of each word on the list and copy the word next to the right letter of the alphabet. Remember, all the words must be written on this list. When you have finished, check for spelling.

A _____
B _____
C _____
D _____
E _____
F _____
G _____
H _____
I _____
J _____
K _____
L _____
M _____
N _____
O _____
P _____
Q _____
R _____
S _____
T _____
U _____
V _____
W _____
X _____
Y _____
Z _____

Which word comes first?

Date _____

alphabet sheet. Does ...t to it? If so, write the ...rst letter of the set of

... felt-tipped ...ond letter.

... felt-tipped ...ond letter.

...n felt-tipped ...nd letter.

...w felt-tipped ...nd letter.

...d letters on it. ... this.

| K | L | M |
| X | Y | Z |

...he first word on ...to the letter 'A'.

...onary.

for support'.) Give out the children's lists of correctly spelled words and remind them to transcribe the words carefully and neatly into their dictionaries. They should pay special attention to the order in which they list the words in their dictionary when more than one word starts with the same letter. Remind them how to do this. On completion, the children should be reminded that the dictionaries can be referred to when they are writing or checking for 'careless mistakes' and that they can also add new words once they can spell them correctly.

Suggestion(s) for extension

Encourage those children who are confident with the alphabet to write all their known words straight into their dictionary without using the photocopiable alphabet sheet. They could then refer back to their list of 'All the words I can nearly spell' (see previous activity). If they have not yet made this list they should do so now. Then they should agree with you on a number of these words which are to be corrected, learned and then entered into their personal

dictionary. The children should first try self-correction strategies such as 'have a go' (that is, writing down three different possible spellings) or use published dictionaries in order to try to locate the correct spelling of the words. Having found the correct spelling, they should memorise the words, for example by using the 'look–cover–write–check' technique, and ask a partner to test them. Once they know the correct spellings, these words can be added to the dictionary.

Suggestion(s) for support

Those children who need support should be given the photocopiable alphabet sheet on page 98 in order to sort out their words into alphabetical order before they embark on transferring their lists into their personal dictionaries. (Photocopiable sheet 99 has a special section for working out the sequence of words that start with the same letter and has a horizontal alphabet.) The photocopiable sheets are intended for rough working, so it does not matter if the children need to cross out or change words. When they have done this, it may be an appropriate point to end the session and then on a subsequent occasion the children could be asked to transcribe the list into their dictionaries.

As they work on the list, the children will probably discover

that they have a set of words that all start with the same letter. They need to understand at this point that the words cannot be listed randomly in the dictionary but that they have to be sorted out into alphabetical order. Since this cannot be decided by the first letter, as it is the same for all the words, then they must look at the second letters. Give the children the second photocopiable sheet (page 99) which is designed to help work out these words. They should first write down the words randomly one under the other in the spaces provided and then, using a different-coloured felt-tipped pen for each word, underline the second letters. Next, ask the children to select coloured counters to match the felt-tipped pen used for each word. Taking each word at a time, they should look at the underlined letter, identify it, locate it on the horizontal alphabet strip and then place the matching coloured counter on the correct letter. In this way the alphabet strip is used to identify the order of the second letters. Ask the child to look at the position of the counters on the horizontal alphabet and decide which counter is nearest to the beginning of the alphabet. Explain to the child that when he writes these words into his personal dictionary the one with the second letter nearest to the beginning must come first because that letter is higher up the sequence than the other second letters. Look at the position of the other counters to confirm this. Which word does the child think will come next? If necessary, ask him to number the words to help him retain the order or he can write the words in the correct sequence in the spaces provided at the bottom of the sheet. Then help him write them into his dictionary.

Assessment opportunities

In this activity the children will demonstrate their confidence in applying their knowledge of the alphabet. They will show this through the way they label their dictionaries with the letters of the alphabet. Some children may still need to refer to alphabet strips and books to help them; note which portions of the alphabet these children are still unsure of. As they begin to enter the words into the dictionary, observe whether this is done automatically or whether the children need to use the supporting strategies provided in the photocopiable sheets. Some children will be able to sort several words which share the same initial letter into their

letter created. Once the frames have been created, children can simply move the cursor to the relevant frame and type in their words.

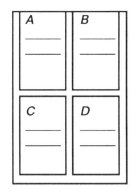

Display ideas
The 'All the words I can spell' books are intended to be for the private use of the children. However, a whole class dictionary could be compiled, entitled 'All the words we can spell' and this could be added to over time.

Aspects of the English PoS covered
Writing – 2b, d, e.

Reference to photocopiable sheets
Photocopiable pages 98 and 99 are to be used for children who need support in compiling their personal dictionaries.

correct sequence automatically, while others will need to use the ideas for support to achieve this.

Opportunities for IT
Individual children could create their own personal dictionary using a word processor or simple desktop publishing package. They could type in their own word list, use the spelling checker to check for mistakes and then print the list out for future reference. The complete list should be saved on a disk, possibly the pupils' own floppy disk, so that they can return at a later date to extend and reprint their list.

Once the list has been compiled, the children could be shown how to use the 'cut and paste' or 'drag and drop' facilities on their word processor to put the list into alphabetical order. There are several ways that the ordered lists could be displayed and printed.

▲ Children could group the words under each letter on the same page. If a word processor is used, this might entail the use of the Tab key or double-column effects to make use of the whole width of the page.

▲ A second option would be to create a page layout so that each new letter could be placed on a different page. Although making the entry simple, this would need at least 26 pages if each letter is to have its own page... quite heavy on paper demands for printing. A smaller format could be used, for example A5, to reduce the printing time and costs.

▲ If a desktop publishing package is used, each page could have, say, four different letters on it and a frame for each

VOWELS AND CONSONANTS

To equip children with essential terminology to enable them to talk analytically about words.

†† *Whole class or small groups.*

⊕ *Total of 45 minutes: 10 minutes introduction; 25 minutes individual work; 10 minutes as a whole group at the end.*

Previous skills/knowledge needed
Children will need to have extensive knowledge of the alphabet and will have had some experience of using the letters of the alphabet when they talk about words. They may have heard the terms 'vowel' and 'consonant' used by the teacher or other pupils.

Key background information
It was the Cox Committee (1989) which recognised the importance of and endorsed the use of linguistic terminology in the English National Curriculum. If children are to understand how language works, they need to be able to talk about it. In order to do this, they require a language with which they can talk about language, known as metalanguage.

'Vowel' and 'consonant' are essential terms that will provide children with a metalanguage with which to talk about the spelling and structure of words. The use of these terms is essential for many of the activities in this book.

Preparation

Make alphabet strips for those who may need them. Make copies of photocopiable pages 100 and 101, each child needing one copy of either of these sheets according to the degree of difficulty experienced. Write the full alphabet on the flip chart and also write the words 'vowel' and 'consonant'. Head the two sheets of paper for the support activity: 'Names that start with a vowel' and 'Names that start with a consonant'. Prepare a list of class names (first names only).

Resources needed

Alphabet strips, dictionaries, alphabet books, photocopiable sheets 100 and 101, pencils, felt-tipped pens, flip chart or chalkboard, rough paper; blank playing-cards for extension activity; two sheets of paper and list of class names for support activity.

What to do

Explain to the whole group that they require two useful terms to help them understand and talk about letters and words. These two terms are called 'vowel' and 'consonant'. Show the class the chart with these terms written down and then ask if they know anything about the two words. Collate their information on the chart. They should identify that the five vowels are 'a', 'e', 'i', 'o' and 'u'. They should then identify the other letters as consonants. Some children will be able to explain that there are five vowels and twenty-one consonants in the alphabet. Review this information by first

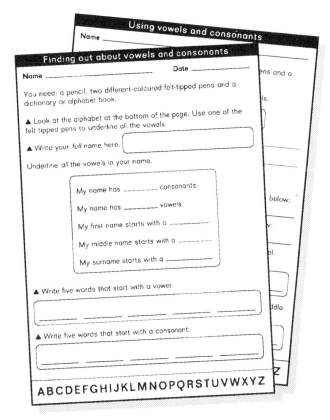

checking that all the group are aware that the alphabet has 26 letters. Next, underline or circle the vowels written on the flip chart and then check that the children recognise that the other letters are known as consonants.

Play a quick quiz, with questions such as 'Is "p" a vowel or a consonant?' This will give time for those who need it to hear the terms in use and to listen to other's responses. Then play a second quick quiz where the children have to think about their own names and respond as rapidly as they can to the questions asked: for example, 'Hands up if your first name starts with a vowel' or 'Hands up if your first name ends in a consonant.' If asked to answer the question directly, the child must reply using the correct terminology, such as 'My name starts with a vowel and ends with a consonant.' This will sharpen the children's knowledge and familiarise them with using the terminology. The quizzes will also enable initial assessments to be made about individual children's needs and the suitability of the worksheets that follow.

The children should then move on to the differentiated photocopiable sheets (photocopiable page 100 for children requiring support work and photocopiable page 101 for children needing extension work) which are intended to check their knowledge and to help them apply it. Leave ten minutes at the end of the session for the children to discuss their findings.

Suggestion(s) for extension

Those children who are confident at identifying and using vowels and consonants can be asked to make some quiz cards for the other children to use. Compile one or two

21

sample cards to provide ideas: for example, 'How many vowels are there in hippopotamus?' or 'Write a one-syllable word which has two vowels.' Another question might be: 'Write a word that is made up only of consonants.' In order to compile the questions the children will need dictionaries. They will need the blank playing-cards to write their questions on and they should make a separate set of answer cards.

Suggestion(s) for support

Some children may still reveal weaknesses in their knowledge of the alphabet. Give them an alphabet strip and highlight the vowels with a pen. Show the children the highlighted

letters on the alphabet strip and remind them that these are the vowels. They should look at the strip to help them as they carry out the activities on the photocopiable sheets.

Give the children two sheets of paper one headed 'Names that start with a vowel' and the other headed 'Names that start with a consonant'. Give them a list (preferably a word-processed one) of all the children's names in the class. Ask the children to reorganise the class list so that it is separated into two lists on the two pieces of paper – one list of names that start with a consonant and one list of names that start with a vowel. Check that they understand which list is which. It might help to write out the vowels on the 'Names that start with a vowel' sheet.

Assessment opportunities

Some children will demonstrate that they understand the terms 'vowel' and 'consonant' and will use the terms when talking about and analysing words. Other children may be able to link vowels and consonants to familiar words, such as their names, but may have more difficulty when talking

about unfamiliar words. Children who are working on the extension activity may discover by actively looking for vowels and consonants that most words have a vowel in each syllable and that very few words have no vowels in them at all.

Opportunities for IT

Children could use a word processor to make extra quiz cards and answers. These could be printed out and mounted on card for other children to use. If children use a simple desktop publishing package they could experiment with different borders and print styles to make their quiz cards more interesting to look at.

Display ideas

Display the quiz cards made in the extension activity, along with a dictionary and rough paper and pencil. If the children use the cards in pairs they can take turns to read the questions and, after trying to reach solutions, supply the answers. (Rules for using the answer cards will need to be clarified.)

The two name charts made in the extension activity can be displayed on the wall or used as rota lists for class monitor jobs.

Aspects of the English PoS covered

Speaking and listening – 2a.
Writing – 2d.

Reference to photocopiable sheets

Photocopiable sheet 100 is designed to help those children who need practice in identifying vowels and consonants. Photocopiable sheet 101 will provide extension work for children who are more confident.

LONG AND SHORT VOWELS

To raise children's awareness that vowels can be long or short and to enable them to talk about this.
†† *Whole class or small groups.*
🕐 *Total of 45 minutes: 20 minutes whole class activity; 15 minutes individual work; 10 minutes whole class.*

Previous skills/knowledge needed

Children will have an extensive knowledge of the alphabet and will have some experience of using the terms 'vowel' and 'consonant' when talking about words. They may have heard the teacher using the terms 'long vowels' and 'short vowels' when discussing distinguishing features of words.

Key background information

Since the English National Curriculum's inception, it has been acknowledged that children require appropriate terminology in order to talk about words and how they work. An interesting

and informative discussion on linguistic terminology was undertaken by Brian Cox (*Cox on Cox: English Curriculum for the 1990s*, Hodder, 1991) which clearly indicates the need for children to be equipped with the appropriate language with which to talk about language (metalanguage). 'Vowel' and 'consonant' are essential terms that children need to be able to use with confidence. In addition, when looking at the curious behaviour of words, such as those with silent 'e' as a final letter, it is essential for teachers to talk to children about the way the vowels work. The key terms in these discussions are 'long vowels' and 'short vowels'.

Preparation

Write the alphabet on the flip chart. Also write the words 'vowel' and 'consonant' and their Latin roots '*vocalis*' (voice) and '*consonare*' (to sound together). Write out the vowels. Photocopy worksheet 102 (one for each child). Collect objects or photographs which have names starting with long or short vowels. It may be easier to focus on one vowel per session, starting with 'a'. (For 'a', short vowel words might include 'apple', 'ant', 'adder', 'animal', 'Africa', and the long vowel words might include 'apron', 'acorn' and 'Asia'.) Prepare alphabet strips for children who need support.

Resources needed

Alphabet strips, dictionaries, alphabet books, photocopiable sheet 102, pencils, felt-tipped pens, flip chart or chalkboard, rough paper, collection of objects which have names starting with long and short vowels; blank playing-cards for extension activity; sheets of good quality A3 paper for support activity.

What to do

For the first ten minutes review the children's existing knowledge of the terms 'vowel' and 'consonant'. Refer to the alphabet which has been written on the flip chart and ask the children to identify the vowels and consonants. Show the class the two words 'vowel' and 'consonant' which have been written on the flip chart. As a brief piece of language study, explain the words' Latin roots (see 'Preparation'). Review the children's existing knowledge by playing a quick quiz which requires them to think about whether words start with vowels or consonants: for example, 'Think of an object that starts with a vowel.' The quiz can become more complex by asking questions such as 'Think of a word that starts with a vowel and ends with a vowel.' Once the children have practised using the terms, move on to the next part of the activity.

Tell the children that in this session they will be thinking about vowels. Draw their attention to the five vowels already written on the flip chart. Find out from the children what they already know about vowels. They may say that most words have them. Some children may comment on the sounds that vowels make. Take one vowel, such as 'a', and show the children a collection of objects (see 'Preparation'). Explain that all the objects start with the same vowel. As you say the names of the items ask the children to listen carefully to the 'a' sound in the words. Start with the short-vowel items and then move on to the long-vowel objects. What do they notice? Can they hear that although all the words start with the 'a' sound, the sound varies? Can they help sort the words according to the sound of the 'a'? With the children's help

sort out the objects. Next, concentrate again on the sound that the 'a' is making but this time focus on helping them verbalise the distinction that they can hear. Can they hear that in 'apron' and 'acorn' the 'a' seems to be saying its letter name? Say the sound slowly and explain that when the vowel 'a' sounds in this way it is behaving as a 'long vowel'. Then repeat the process with the other set of objects and focus on the fact that 'a' in these words is a shorter sound so the vowel 'a' is described as being a 'short vowel'.

Go on to explain that short and long vowel 'a's can occur in different places in words, not just at the beginning. Give some examples, write them on the flip chart and ask the children to listen and try to identify whether the 'a' is behaving as a long or a short vowel. A suitable set of words might be 'age', 'have', 'save', 'shall'. Ask the children to work in pairs, using rough paper, and sort the set of words into two lists – one containing the short-vowel 'a' words and one containing the long-vowel 'a' words. Compare their findings and summarise on the flip chart.

The class should then move on to the individual work on the copies of photocopiable page 102 provided. Allow 15 minutes for this. Then ask the children to pair up and share their work and present one key point from their findings. (The children may find it more supportive the first time they try this activity to work on the sheet in pairs.)

To conclude the session, play a quick quiz where the children can practise using the terminology by posing questions to the class: for example, 'Does 'lane' have a long or a short "a" in it?'

The activity can be repeated on subsequent occasions with a focus on different vowels.

Suggestion(s) for extension

Those children who show a clear understanding of the main activity can compile some quiz cards for the other children to use. An example might be: Does the word 'ant' have a long or short 'a' at the beginning? A more challenging example might be 'odd one out' cards, such as 'Read these words: cat, fat, lane, rat. Which is the odd one out? Does it have a long vowel or a short vowel in the middle?'

The solutions would be written on 'answer cards'. The

children may need dictionaries to help them. They will require blank playing-cards to write their questions and answers on.

Suggestion(s) for support

For children who found the main activity challenging, provide an alphabet strip and ask them to identify the vowels by highlighting them. Check their existing knowledge of vowels. Can they think of names of objects which have initial letters starting with any of the vowel letters? Collect their responses.

Then using the set of short 'a' objects, ask the children to name the objects. Can they think of some more words that start with a short 'a'? (Encourage them to include names on this list, including family, friends, pets and pop groups.) Using a sheet of good quality A3 drawing paper write a heading: 'All these people and things start with a short "a".' The children should choose four things to draw and label.

Assessment opportunities

In the main activity the children will reveal their confidence in using the terms 'vowel' and 'consonant'. In the quizzes they will also demonstrate their ability to apply that knowledge with varying degrees of complexity. Sorting the long and short vowel objects will indicate children's growing auditory skills and their increasing ability to distinguish the sounds.

Some children may comment that other combinations of letters can make the long 'a' sound, for example 'ai' and 'ei' words. Through the final quiz and in the extension activities, the children will make explicit use of their linguistic terminology.

Some children may reveal a very limited understanding, perhaps succeeding only in sorting the sound when working with the objects.

Opportunities for IT

Children could use a word processor to make extra quiz cards and answers. These could be printed out and mounted on card for other children to use. If children use a simple desktop publishing package they could experiment with different borders and print styles to make their quiz cards more interesting.

Where classes have access to talking word processors children might explore the long and short vowel sounds in a

range of words which can be entered at the keyboard. Children will need to be shown how to turn on the speech effect, selecting individual words for listening. The quality of the speech produced does vary and the activity might raise the issue of the effectiveness of computer generated speech in obeying the rules of pronunciation.

An alternative approach would be to use the speech from a story-based CD-ROM which is often sampled human speech saved in digital form on the disk. Children could explore the different vowel sounds from a story CD-ROM where it is usually possible to select and listen to an individual word. They could work in pairs, selecting a word, deciding on the vowel sound, then listening to the word spoken and checking their original answer. More able children might be able to set up a simple quiz using the CD-ROM by identifying 20 words representing different types of vowel sounds, on different pages of the story-book, and providing the answer for other children. The activity would give pupils opportunities to explore the CD-ROM and to learn how to move around the pages.

Display ideas

The quiz cards and answer cards from the extension activity could form part of an interactive display. The cards will be most successful if used in pairs. (Set up ground rules for the use of the answer cards.) The chart made in the support activity could form part of a wall display which can be added to over time. Write a heading for the display – 'All about long and short vowels'.

Aspects of the English PoS covered

Speaking and listening – 2a.
Writing – 2d.

Reference to photocopiable sheet

Photocopiable sheet 102 is for individual work after the initial class discussion on long and short vowels. Children could work on it in pairs, if preferred.

FROM WORD BANK TO DICTIONARY

To enable children to construct a simple dictionary.
†† *Four children, working in pairs.*
🕐 *1 hour.*

Previous skills/knowledge needed

Children will be able to read and write the alphabet and will have some experience of using wordbooks and simple dictionaries. They will be accustomed to using 'word banks' to help them in topic work.

Key background information

It is important for children to be able to use published dictionaries but their attempts are frequently thwarted by not being able to find the 'right' word. Teachers find word banks one way of combating this problem but, helpful though they may be, word banks are not necessarily organised in alphabetical order, nor do they provide children with systematic practice of essential dictionary skills. Word banks can, however, form a supportive starting point for children to learn how to construct and use a dictionary. By utilising a familiar set of words which the class have brainstormed to form a word bank, the teacher can then help the children make their own topic-based dictionaries. In doing this, the

SPELLING AND PHONICS KS2

children are learning from the inside how a dictionary works. They will need to consider the organisation of the book, how to use the full alphabetic sequence and the problem of organising several words which start with the same initial letter and why this is important later on when the dictionary is used.

The following activity is designed for four children working in two pairs, but it could also be undertaken on an individual basis so that everyone has their own dictionary.

Preparation

To make the book, fold the seven sheets of A3 paper in half and place them one inside the other so that they look like a book. Take a needle and thread and sew a figure of eight to hold the pages together (see figure 1). Measure the length of one of the A4 boards and measure the same amount of bookbinding tape plus a little extra at both ends. Cut the tape and lay it flat on the table (adhesive side up). Take the two boards and lie them close together on the adhesive tape, but not quite touching each other, leaving enough room at both ends so that the tape can be turned over to secure the inside of the boards (see figure 2). Cover the boards with coloured paper. Take the pages which have been sewn together, open the pages at the centre and turn them face down flat on the table. Cover the 'end papers' thoroughly with glue. Then, holding the sewn pages as if opening a book, position the fold carefully in between the two boards so that the spine is sitting on the exposed adhesive strip. Carefully position the first 'end paper' against one of the boards and

press firmly and then repeat the process with the other 'end paper' (see figure 3). Press out all creases and allow the book to dry. (The bookmaking could be undertaken by the group of children prior to the session as a design and technology activity.)

Prepare a word bank by selecting a class topic and brainstorming with the children all the words they think they might need to know. (See also the photocopiable word bank sheet on page 103 based on the topic of the Victorians which is designed for the extension activity but could be used in the main activity if a word bank is unavailable.) Prepare an alphabet sheet by taking a sheet of A4 paper and writing the letters of the alphabet down the left-hand side of the page in a column.

Prepare individual dictionaries for those who will be working on the extension activity. For the support activity prepare a zigzag book by cutting a length of card, making 26 equal-sized folds and labelling them with the letters of the alphabet. Prepare the alphabet strip.

Resources needed

Materials to make an A4-size book – boards for the covers, seven sheets of A3 paper, glue, coloured paper for cover, bookbinding tape, needle, thread; word bank or photocopiable page 103; reference books on chosen topic; pens, pencils, drawing materials; published dictionaries and alphabets; a sheet of A4 paper with the alphabet written down one side; small individual notebooks for extension activity; alphabet strip, flip chart, drawing paper, writing paper, large piece of coloured card for zigzag book for support activity.

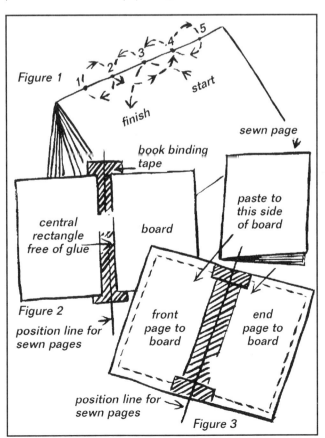

Figure 1

sewn page

book binding tape

paste to this side of board

central rectangle free of glue

board

Figure 2

position line for sewn pages

front page to board

end page to board

position line for sewn pages

Figure 3

What to do

Talk to the children about how and why the class word bank was made. (If a suitable word bank is unavailable, then photocopiable sheet 103 could be used.) Explain that although the word bank is useful the words could be better organised, for example by putting them into a class dictionary. Ask the children what the advantages of doing this are. It is important that they recognise that the alphabetic sequence can help us gain speedy access to the word we are looking for. Next ask them what they would need to do in order to turn the word bank into a class dictionary. They should identify the need for a dictionary with 26 pages. They should also suggest that each page of the dictionary is labelled with the appropriate letter of the alphabet. Use a published dictionary to illustrate these points.

Introduce the ready-made blank dictionary and identify the tasks for the group. The first job will be for one pair to work through the letters of the alphabet and to take turns to label the pages. (It will be necessary to use the inside of the back papers in order to fit each of the 26 letters on to a separate page.) The children should write the letters neatly, in pencil first of all in case they make errors. While they are doing this, the second pair should look at the class word bank (or use the sample word bank on photocopiable page 103) and then, using the alphabet sheet as a rough draft, reorganise the words so that they are in their alphabetic

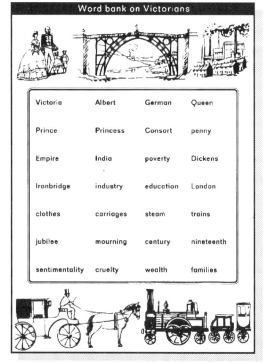

Word bank on Victorians			
Victoria	Albert	German	Queen
Prince	Princess	Consort	penny
Empire	India	poverty	Dickens
Ironbridge	industry	education	London
clothes	carriages	steam	trains
jubilee	mourning	century	nineteenth
sentimentality	cruelty	wealth	families

sequence. If the first pair finish first, they can compose a title for the dictionary and carefully write this on the book cover, perhaps with an illustration.

Once the rough list is complete, review it with *both* pairs and focus on any letters that have two or more entries. Ask the second pair to try to explain how they decided the order of these words. Then ask the first pair whether they agree. The aim here is to get the children to explain that when more than one word starts with the same initial letter its order is determined by the position of the second letter in the alphabetic sequence. If the second letters are the same, then it is necessary to look at the third. If the children cannot explain this, then use a simple published dictionary and the alphabet strip to explain this organisational device to them. Sort out the order of the words and then ask the children to take turns in pairs to transfer the list into the class dictionary. Divide the list as fairly as possible into approximately four parts. Ask the first pair to work on the first quarter and then swap over with the second pair who will work on the second quarter. They should swap again in order to complete the dictionary. While one pair is working on the dictionary the other pair can work on small illustrations to accompany some of the words. The children could also write short definitions of some of the words. When the dictionary is complete, read it through together. Identify pages that do not have an entry yet and

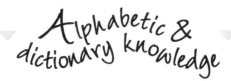

then look for pages that have plenty of entries. Explain that the dictionary is now ready for use to help them with their writing and that additional entries can be made as they progress.

Suggestion(s) for extension

At the end of the main activity play a short quiz in which the children have to answer as quickly as possible where they think words can be found. For example, if the teacher says, 'Where should I look for "beetle"?' the children should say, 'Near the beginning.' Ask them to guess where to open the book in order to find different words. If the photocopiable word bank sheet was not used in the main activity this can now be used as an extension activity. Give out the individual dictionaries and ask the children to label them with the alphabet. Then give out copies of the photocopiable word bank sheet (page 103). Ask the children to sort the words into their individual dictionaries. (The sheet includes several words that start with the same letter.) Give the children the alphabet sheet for rough working.

Suggestion(s) for support

Some children may still find handling the pages of a dictionary very difficult and may display weaknesses in their alphabetic knowledge. The class dictionary could be specially adapted with 'tabs' that stick out indicating where the letters can be found. Alternatively, these children might cope better if they make a dictionary in the form of a zigzag book. Ask them to read the word bank aloud and identify words that they can recognise on sight. These should be the words that are used first in the zigzag book. Use the alphabet sheet to help the children think about where the words fit into the sequence. The children should then write the words on the appropriate page of the zigzag book and illustrate the words entered. More words can be added as the children become familiar with them. To help the children consider the ordering of words that start with the same initial sound, ask them to suggest three words that start with the same initial letter. Write these on the flip chart and then discuss their order by looking at the second letters. Stick the alphabet strip across the bottom of the flip chart for the children to refer to.

Assessment opportunities

In the main activity, observe how successfully the children manage to write the alphabet into the dictionary. How well did they take the words from the word bank and sort these into sequence on the alphabet sheet? Did they understand how to sequence words that start with the same initial letter?

As children write the words into the dictionary, it is interesting to note whether they are able to skip pages that are redundant or whether they need to run through the whole sequence. Their responses during the quiz will indicate their growing flexibility with handling the alphabet and their awareness of where letters fall in the sequence.

Opportunities for IT

A word processor or desktop publishing package could be used for children to make their topic word bank. A master format for the dictionary could be created, with a page for each letter of the alphabet. Once the word list has been decided, children could type in the words on the appropriate pages, possibly working in pairs on one or two pages.

It might be possible to add illustrations, either for the letter of the page or selected words, by creating or selecting pictures in keeping with the theme of the word bank. Children could use a simple art or drawing package to create their own illustrations, or could select pictures from an appropriate CD-ROM or collection of theme-based clip art. This would give them an opportunity to combine two different sorts of information on a single page, sizing and positioning the pictures to fit the page.

In order to update the list, children could either write new words on the printed pages, stick on new words printed from the original software, possibly on sticky labels, or reprint individual pages with new words added. The latter approach would mean that the full word bank would need to be printed on loose-leaf pages so that individual pages could be added and amended as needed. They could be displayed in transparent sleeves. It would provide an opportunity to discuss with the children the advantages and disadvantages of using IT for this kind of work.

Display ideas

The class dictionary and the zigzag book can be placed alongside books on the class topic or in the section of the class library which contains dictionaries and alphabet books.

Aspects of the English PoS covered

Speaking and listening – 1a.
Reading – 1b; 2c.
Writing – 2d.

Reference to photocopiable sheet

Photocopiable sheet 103 can be used as an alternative to a class word bank.

FIND THAT LETTER

To enable children to locate efficiently initial letters in the dictionary.

†† *Groups of four, working in two pairs.*

🕘 *20 minutes.*

Previous skills/knowledge needed

Children will have had experience of utilising their alphabetic knowledge in the organising and making of simple dictionaries. They will have begun to establish the link between the initial letters of words and the location of these words in the dictionary. They may still be developing their knowledge of which part of the dictionary they should go to in order to find the initial letter of the word.

Key background information

In order to find a dictionary useful, children need to understand the basics about how it works. Most dictionaries they will be required to use in school will be organised alphabetically and within each alphabetical segment words are yet again organised alphabetically. Children need plenty of practice at working on these two areas in order to use dictionaries efficiently. They have to discover that, unlike a story-book, when reading a dictionary it is unproductive to start at the beginning and end at the end. The child has to learn to judge which portion of the book to look at initially and then expect to adjust this first look by moving either backwards or forwards through the pages. Without a sound knowledge of the alphabet, this can quickly become frustrating.

Preparation

You will need to buy a blank deck of cards or, if that is too expensive, you can make a template of four blank playing-cards. In order to make a set of alphabet cards, make seven photocopies, which will leave two spare cards. The photocopies should then be mounted on to the A1 card. Using a dark-coloured felt-tipped pen, clearly write a single letter of the alphabet on each card so that you have a complete set of alphabet cards. If possible, laminate the cards and then cut them out. The deck of cards is now ready. Prepare the alphabet strips by writing the alphabet horizontally. Enough of these should be made to ensure that each pair of children can see one. Provide one copy of photocopiable sheet 104 for each pair.

Resources needed

A selection of dictionaries and alphabet books, 26 blank playing-cards (see 'Preparation'), A1 sheets of thin card in one colour, A4 paper, pencils, dark-coloured felt-tipped pen, alphabet strips, glue, scissors, laminating material, photocopiable sheet 104.

SPELLING AND PHONICS KS2

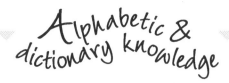

What to do

First show the children the dictionaries or alphabet books that they will be working with. Ask them to explain why dictionaries are useful and how they are organised. If the children do not comment on the alphabetic nature of the organisation, draw their attention to it. Then ask the children how they would find a word in the dictionary. Again they should indicate the initial letter as being the key point of entry. Demonstrate this for them by asking them to suggest a letter. Use the alphabet strip to decide whether the letter comes near the beginning, middle or end of the alphabet and then look for the appropriate section in the dictionary. Let each child practise finding an initial letter of her choice in the dictionary, focusing on the idea of beginning, middle and end, and encourage them to use the alphabet strip to help them.

Now explain that the purpose of the activity is to speed up their skill at finding different initial letters in the dictionary as this will also help them in the future when they want to find a particular word. Organise the two pairs into teams called Team One and Team Two. Each child in the pair is to call themselves either 'A' or 'B'. In the first round of the activity child 'A' in both teams will start; in the second round child 'B' will take the lead. This pattern continues until the end of the activity.

Give each pair a copy of the same dictionary or alphabet book. Start by showing the children the deck of alphabet cards, shuffle them and place them on the table. Explain that they are going to take turns to take the top card off the deck. Child 'A' in the team sitting to the right of the teacher will start the game. Play a demonstration round first. For example, ask the child to pick up the first card on the deck, look at it and then say to child 'A' on the opposite team, 'Can you find the "C" pages in the dictionary?' That child should then try to find the "C" section in the dictionary as quickly as she can. If she can find the section, she must show it to the group and then if she is correct she should keep the "C" card. If the answer is incorrect, the opposite team takes a turn to locate the letter in their dictionary. If they succeed, then they retain the alphabet card. The game continues until all the cards have been collected. At the end of the game, the children should identify any letters that they found difficult and try those again.

Suggestion(s) for extension

As the children play the game they can use the photocopiable self-evaluation sheet (page 104) to record their progress. The player who is not leading the team's round records his partner's progress and vice versa. At the end of the game, the children can use the sheet themselves to identify the letters with which they need more practice.

Suggestion(s) for support

Children who find working with a dictionary too difficult should use an alphabet book. Many of these are more sophisticated

Find that letter: how did you do?		
Name _____ Date _____		
▲ Use this sheet as you play the game to note how you got on.		
Suggestions for what you could write: It was hard/easy, couldn't find right page, lost my place, I was too slow.		
Team members' names: _____ _____		
Write the letter below:	Write your comments:	
	☺ We did well	☹ We had problems

**SPELLING AND
PHONICS KS2**

in their graphics and content and thus more suitable for Key Stage 2 children. If the children do not remember to refer to the alphabet strip as an intermediary step in finding the right section of the book, remind them to do so. Remind them also that if they open the dictionary in the wrong place they should consult the alphabet strip to help them decide whether to move forwards or backwards. Give further demonstrations of the position of letters at the beginning, middle or end of the alphabet and link this back to the dictionaries or alphabet books. If necessary, look at the alphabet strip with the children and cut it into three sections which are identified as the 'beginning letters', the 'middle letters' and the 'end letters'. Although this can only be a rough guide, it will help the children develop their judgement.

Assessment opportunities

In this activity the children will demonstrate their growing confidence in being able to locate initial letters in the dictionary or alphabet book. Some children will be able to open the book at different points and others will need to run through the whole alphabet in sequence. If children open the dictionary at the incorrect point can they judge whether to move forwards or backwards to find the letter they are seeking?

Aspects of the English PoS covered

Speaking and listening – 1a.
Reading – 1b.
Writing – 2d.

Reference to photocopiable sheet

The self-evaluation sheet (photocopiable page 104) can be used as part of the extension activity.

FIND THAT WORD

To enable children to find common words in the dictionary.
†† *Groups of four, working in two pairs.*
🕐 *30 minutes.*

Previous skills/knowledge needed

Pupils will have had practice at utilising their alphabetic knowledge in order to look for specific sections in the dictionary. They will have considered whether certain initial letters are more likely to appear near the beginning, middle or end of the book. If they open the book in the wrong place, they will have drawn on their knowledge of the alphabet to decide whether they should go forwards or backwards in order to find the correct place. They will have had some experience of ordering words that start with the same initial sound by looking at subsequent letters. They will have had some practice at looking for specific words in published dictionaries, although this is not essential.

Key background information

Children need to learn how to make dictionaries work for them. They need to discover that dictionaries are organised alphabetically. In order to make sense of this organisational system they must learn to look beyond the initial letter of a word to the subsequent letters and discover that they too are sequenced alphabetically. The shift of focus to subsequent letters can prove problematic if the children are unclear about what the second letter might be. Their existing phonic knowledge will assist them in this, as will their knowledge of 'onset' and 'rime' (see 'Phonological aspects

of learning to read' in *Teaching Literacy, Balancing Perspectives* by Roger Beard, Hodder, 1993).

Preparation

The 52 blank playing-cards will be used as word cards with two common words for each letter of the alphabet represented on the cards. If it is too expensive to buy two decks of blank playing-cards, photocopy the template you made for the previous activity 'Find that letter'. Mount the photocopies on to thin card (do not cut the cards out at this stage). For the word cards choose two common words for each letter of the alphabet, each having a different second letter, and ensure that they occur in the dictionaries that will be used. Using a dark-coloured felt-tipped pen, write one word on each card. Once the set is complete, all 52 cards should have a word on, representing the full range of the alphabet. Each initial letter should occur twice. Now laminate the sheets and cut the cards out. Make one alphabet strip for each pair. If children are working with the self-evaluation activity described in the 'Suggestion(s) for extension', make one copy of photocopiable page 105 for each team.

Resources needed

A deck of 52 blank playing-cards (see 'Preparation'), alphabet books or dictionaries, alphabet strips, laminating material, felt-tipped pens, A1 sheets of thin card, photocopiable page 105 for extension activity.

What to do

First show the children the dictionaries or alphabet books that they will be working with. Review their knowledge of how dictionaries work and how they are organised. If they do not comment on the alphabetic nature of the organisation, then draw their attention to this. Ask the children how they would go about finding a word in the dictionary. It is likely that they will refer to the initial letter as being the key. Ask the children to suggest an initial letter to look for. If they say 'b', for example, use one of the alphabet strips for guidance as to whether the letter is at the beginning, middle or towards the end of the dictionary. Once the 'b' section is found, ask the children to suggest a common word starting with 'b' and then explain how to find the word. Establish that there are lots of words that start with 'b' in this section of the dictionary

and that in order to find the chosen word (let's say, 'broom') it is necessary to try to identify the next letter. Ask what the next letter might be. Guide them by drawing attention to the onset 'br'. Once 'r' is identified, explain that in order to find words easily in the dictionary, the second letters are also organised alphabetically. The group must therefore think about the position of 'r' in the alphabet. At this point use the alphabet strip to support or confirm the decisions. Then demonstrate to the children how to run through the second letters of the 'b' words alphabetically. Identify the 'br' section and focus on the rime 'oom'. What sound can they hear in 'oom'? Looking out for the 'oom' rime, run down the 'br' words until 'broom' is found.

Tell the children that they are going to play a game. Explain that the purpose of the game is to help them practise finding words in the dictionary. Organise the two pairs into teams called Team One and Team Two. Each child in the pair is to be called either 'A' or 'B'. In the first round of the activity, child 'A' in Team One will start the game. In the second round child 'A' in Team Two takes the lead. Then child 'B' in each team takes a turn to lead. This will be the pattern until the end of the activity. Give each team a copy of the same dictionary or alphabet book. Next, introduce the word cards, using 26 of them for the first time that the game is played (ensure that each letter of the alphabet is represented). Show the children the cards and explain that there are word cards for every letter of the alphabet. Shuffle the cards. Starting with child 'A' in Team One, explain that they are going to take turns to pick a word card off the top of the pack and ask the opposite team to find the word in their dictionary or alphabet book. (The opposing team can work together to locate the words.) If the opposing team manage to find the word, they keep the card. If they cannot locate it, the other team has a chance. If they find the word, they keep the card.

Use the first round to review all the points already made. Ask the first player to take a word card off the top of the deck. Child 'A' might say, 'Sean, can you find the word "shop"?' Sean should then open the dictionary at the 's' pages and search for the word. If he fails to locate the 's' pages, draw his attention to the idea of 'beginning', 'middle' and 'end' of the alphabet. Use the alphabet strip to help him. Once the correct initial letter is located, remind him about

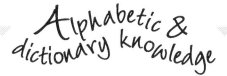

saying the word aloud in order to try to listen for the second letter. In this case the focus will be on the consonant digraph 'sh'. If he can find the word, he retains the card. The word should be shown to the opposing team. If he is unsuccessful, the team that asked the question can look for the word. The game continues until all the word cards have been won. If the children encounter any problem words, these should be placed in a separate pile until the end and then looked at again.

Suggestion(s) for extension

Using all 52 cards, the children can play as individuals. The complexity of the game can be developed by making sets of cards with words that require the child to attend closely to third, fourth and subsequent letters: examples might be 'hand' and 'handle' or 'signal' and 'signature'. These children can also use photocopiable page 105 as a self-evaluation sheet to record their progress in the game.

Suggestion(s) for support

Some children will be more successful if they work with an alphabet book, rather than a dictionary. There are plenty of published alphabets that meet the needs and interests of Key Stage 2 children – for example, 'The Calypso Alphabet' by John Agard (Picture Lions, 1993), 'Animalia' by Graeme Base (Puffin, 1990), 'A is for Africa' by Ifeoma Onyefulu (Frances Lincoln, 1993), 'I Could Have Been...' by Dennis Longmore (Teachers for Travellers, 1990). Use one deck of

26 cards with this group and ensure that the words on the cards are familiar.

Assessment opportunities

The children will demonstrate their increasing knowledge of the alphabet by the way they locate letters in the dictionary. Some children will still need to refer to the alphabet strip for help. They will demonstrate their understanding of looking at the alphabetic sequence of letters in words by the way that they talk about the sounds they can hear in the words and by their method of tracking second letters in the dictionary. The rate of success in finding the words will be another obvious indicator. Evidence for this can be gathered from the self-evaluation sheets (photocopiable page 105) completed by the children.

Display ideas

The game can be displayed for other children to use on future occasions.

Aspects of the English PoS covered

Speaking and listening – 1c.
Reading – 2c.
Writing – 2d.

Reference to photocopiable sheet

The self-evaluation sheet (photocopiable page 105) can be used by those children who show confidence in locating words in the dictionary.

Find that word: how did you do?

Name _____ Date _____

▲ Use this sheet as you play the game to note how you got on.

Suggestions for what you could write: hard, easy, couldn't find letter, lost my place, not sure.

Team members' names: _____ _____

Write the word below:	Write your comments:	
	☺ We did well	☹ We had problems

FIND THAT HEADWORD

To enable children to understand the purpose of headwords in dictionaries and how to use them.

†† *Whole class, then groups of four working in pairs.*

🕐 *Total of 1 hour: 10 minutes whole group, 15 minutes to play the card game in teams; 15 minutes whole group; 20 minutes small groups for extension and support activities.*

Previous skills/knowledge needed

Children will need to have had plenty of experience of applying their knowledge of the alphabet in the organising and making of simple dictionaries. They will have a developing knowledge of where approximately they can locate specific letters of the alphabet in a dictionary: for example, they will have considered whether letters are likely to occur at the beginning, middle or end of the book. They will have looked for words using initial and subsequent letters as a point of reference. Some children may have found this difficult, particularly when relying on subsequent letters.

Key background information

Finding words in dictionaries can be made much less frustrating if children have the organisational devices explained to them and are taught how to use them. While children recognise that dictionaries are organised alphabetically and realise that focusing on the beginning of the word is important, it is easy for them to lose their place when scanning the columns of print and this becomes time wasting if they are

looking in completely the wrong place. The headwords that are usually found at the top of each page in a dictionary are there to tell children the first word and the last word on that page. If the child is looking for a word, particularly in a larger dictionary, it will help them if they can be taught to look at the headwords first, before searching for the word. In order to do this successfully, they must have an approximate idea of the spelling of the word and a thorough working knowledge of the sequence of the alphabet which will enable them to judge whether the word will fit alphabetically in between the two headwords on the page. This is a sophisticated skill and will take a great deal of practice on the part of the child and repeated explanation from the teacher. (The following activity has been based on the layout of headwords in a standard dictionary. It may therefore be necessary to adapt examples and explanations if the dictionaries you are using have different layouts.)

Preparation

If you use the template of blank playing-cards you made for the previous two activities 'Find that letter' and 'Find that word' to make the cards, take three photocopies and mount them on the A1 card. Decide which dictionaries the children will be working with (both pairs of children should have the same dictionary) and select 12 pairs of headwords drawn from across the full range of the alphabet. (12 is an arbitrary choice which should be enough to give the children practice in looking for headwords in the dictionary. All 26 letters could be represented if desired.) Use a dark-coloured

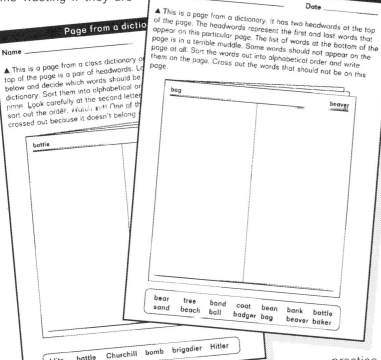

SPELLING AND PHONICS KS2

felt-tipped pen to write the selected pairs of headwords on the cards. Laminate the cards and then cut them out. Prepare an alphabet strip for each pair of children. For the main activity photocopy and enlarge one page from the dictionary and mount this on to A3-size card. For the extension activity make two photocopies of sheet 106. For the support activity photocopy sheet 107 for each child who needs it.

Resources needed

A selection of dictionaries and alphabet books which use headwords at the top of each page, 12 blank playing-cards (see 'Preparation'), felt-tipped pens, alphabet strips, A1 sheets of thin card, scissors, glue, laminating material, photocopiable pages 106 and 107, flip chart or chalkboard, rough paper, one thin felt-tipped pen for each team.

What to do

Show the children some familiar alphabet books and dictionaries and ask them to explain why dictionaries are useful and how they are organised. The children should comment on the alphabetic nature of the organisation, but if they fail to do so then their attention should be drawn to it. Talk about the ways in which they currently find words in the dictionary. It is likely that they will suggest looking for the first letter or initial sound. Some children may know that words can also be found by looking at the second and subsequent letters.

Place the enlarged photocopied page from the dictionary on the flip chart stand. Ask the children to open their own dictionaries at the same page. Provide guidance to enable them to do this. Ask them to look at the two words in bold print at the top of the page and see if they can explain why they think the words are there. If nobody can suggest a reason, ask the children to read the two words aloud and then to look carefully at the first word in the first column and then the last word in the second column on the page. The children should then understand the function of the headwords. Explain that the headwords are there to provide a quick way of checking whether the dictionary has been opened in approximately the right place to find a particular word. Give some examples, using words that appear on the enlarged page, and explain how the headwords can be used to guide the reader who wants to find a word quickly. Then give an example of a word that would clearly not belong between the two headwords. Ask the children to skim through the dictionary and they will notice that all the pages have two words at the top and two columns of print underneath.

Before starting the next part of the activity, check that each pair of children has an alphabet strip and a dictionary (which must be the same for both pairs). Then name the pairs as Team One and Team Two. Each member of the pair must identify themselves as 'A' or 'B'. Show the children the pack of 12 'headword cards' which should be shuffled and placed in the centre of the table. Explain that the aim of this short game is for each pair to take one card off the pile and place it on the table so that they can both read it. They should read the two headwords and find the matching page in their dictionary. They must do this as quickly as they can. As soon as one team thinks they have found the correct page the round comes to an immediate halt. They must show the opposing team that the card and the page match. If the match is correct, the round ends and the winning team keep their card. The opposing team must put their card back at the bottom of the pile. However, if, on checking, an error has been made, the card is returned to the bottom of the pile. The opposing team then has the chance to finish looking for their page in the dictionary. The children should retain the cards that they have successfully matched. The team with the most cards at the end of the game wins. In the first round the cards are picked up 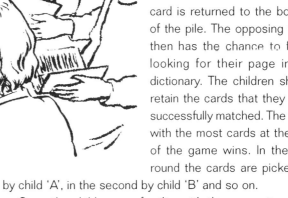 by child 'A', in the second by child 'B' and so on.

Once the children are familiar with the game, it can be made more complex in subsequent rounds – for example, by requiring the children to note down on rough paper one word from each page of the dictionary that they locate by means of the 'headword cards'.

Suggestion(s) for extension

To increase the children's understanding of the organisation and purpose of headwords, use photocopiable sheet 106. This sheet consists of a simplified page from a dictionary. It has two headwords and then a random set of words that may or may not belong on the page. (To simplify the activity, the definitions of the words are not included.) Give each pair a copy of the sheet to look at together.

SPELLING AND PHONICS KS2

First of all remind the children about the role of headwords. On this sheet, 'bag' will be the first word to appear on that particular page of the dictionary and 'beaver' will be the last word. The children will need to decide whether or not all the words on the random list should be included on this page in the dictionary. They must also decide on the correct ordering of the words. If words are rejected from the page the children must justify their decisions. Before they start, remind them to think carefully about the headwords. Both words start with 'b' so only words with the initial letter 'b' on the random list are eligible. Any words that do not start with 'b' can immediately be discounted. But not only must they think about the initial letters, they must also pay attention to the subsequent letters. Point out that in 'bag' the second letter is 'a' and in 'beaver' the second letter is 'e'. Check that they understand why the word 'bag' comes before the word 'beaver'. Their task is now to consider the possible range of second letters that could come in between the two words. (Use the alphabet strips to help the children think about this.) Repeat the procedure with the third letter if deemed necessary. Remind the children as they work with the photocopiable sheet to keep checking their ideas against the alphabet strip and by using their dictionaries. As they work they may use the felt-tipped pens to underline or 'code' letters and to make marks on the alphabet strip. Allow 15 minutes for independent working and then ask the two pairs to compare their findings.

Suggestion(s) for support
For children who found the main activity challenging, photocopiable sheet 107 will provide a highly structured task, focusing on a single page of an imaginary class dictionary. Two headwords are given at the top of the page, with a small word bank of randomly listed words below. (This is based on World War Two.)

The children's task is to try to sort the words into the right order on the blank page of the dictionary. One very obvious 'rogue' word has been included in the list which the children should decide to reject. The words have been carefully chosen so that the children do not have to look beyond the second letters to make their decisions. They will probably need to be reminded about looking at the second letters and using the alphabet strips to help them. If they give each letter a colour code they can underline the second letters in different-coloured pens and then map the second letters on to the alphabet strip. By distinguishing the colours, the children should then be able to look at the alphabetical strip in order to sort the words out.

Assessment opportunities
Children will demonstrate through what they say whether they understand the function of headwords in dictionaries. Do they realise that the pairs of words indicate the first and last word to appear on a page? Note how successful they are during the card game at locating different pairs of headings in the dictionary. This will demonstrate confidence in their alphabetic knowledge. Do they recognise that to start with the initial letter is not enough to make an informed decision about whether a word can belong on a particular page? Do the children make successful judgements about the subsequent letters in order to make decisions about including or excluding words? Record the self-help strategies that children employ, such as referring to alphabet strips.

Display ideas
Display the 'headword card' game for other children to use. Perhaps the children could make their own sets of 'headword cards'. To help children become familiar with the use of headwords, a class topic dictionary could be compiled and organised under headwords.

Aspects of the English PoS covered
Speaking and listening – 2a.
Reading – 1b.
Writing – 2d.

Reference to photocopiable sheets
Photocopiable sheet 106 is intended for use with the extension activity and sheet 107 with the support activity. Both sheets provide pages from a dictionary which the children can fill in with the correct words.

SPELLING AND
PHONICS KS2

MAKING PERSONAL SPELLING BOOKS

To create a way of recording information about spelling and making a reference resource relevant to the individual child. To introduce terminology about spelling and words.

†† *Whole class.*

⏱ *30–45 minutes to make up the booklet.*

Previous skills/knowledge needed

The word lists made in the activity 'All the words I can spell' on page 16 could be incorporated into this book if desired. The children should have had some experience of making their own books for a variety of purposes.

Key background information

As indicated in the introduction to this book, children will be at different stages of development in their spelling skills right through Key Stage 2. It will rarely be possible for an activity to be undertaken by the whole class because the needs of individuals will be different at any given time. Teachers will need to be aware of what each child or small group needs, through observation of their spelling strategies and through noting the spelling errors appearing in the children's writing. If each child has her own spelling book it can be used to record knowledge and spellings learned and will provide a valuable point of reference to remind her of what she does know. The intention, in making this spelling book together, is to use it as a teaching context for the appropriate terminology and to ensure that children know how the booklet is organised. The sections in the booklet follow very closely the Key Skills indicated in the National Curriculum Programme of Study for Spelling.

Preparation

Ready-made notebooks could be used, provided they have enough pages, or little booklets could be made by folding A4 paper in half, providing a coloured paper cover and stapling the spine. The booklet will need 26 *double* pages at the beginning (one for each letter of the alphabet), followed by six to eight single pages for each of the following sections:

▲ spelling rules;
▲ ways of remembering spellings – mnemonics;
▲ silent letters;
▲ prefixes and suffixes;
▲ word families;
▲ words about spelling;
▲ notes/interesting things about words.

The total number of pages will therefore be 68 or 82.

Resources needed

A notebook (see 'Preparation') for each child, pencils, a selection of different-coloured felt-tipped pens, rulers.

What to do

Give out the prepared booklets. Ask the children to write their names and the title 'My Spelling Book' on the cover. Leaving aside the first single page (you will return to this later to make a contents page), on the first double page ask the children to write the letter 'a' in upper and lower case forms (A, a) on the right-hand page, in the top right-hand corner. (This is so that the page headings are more easily seen when children are looking through for particular pages.) Then ask them to write the number 1 at the bottom of this page, in the right-hand corner. They should continue through the book, writing the appropriate letter and number on each page (see below).

When the children reach the first double page after 'z', ask them to write the heading 'spelling rules' at the top of the right-hand page in a different colour from the one they used for the letters. The heading should be underlined using a ruler. Count on three or four double pages (depending on how many you decide to use), then ask the children to write the next heading (see 'Preparation'). Continue in this way until all seven headings have been written, using a different colour for each heading. The last few pages should be left blank for notes about interesting spelling facts. As each of the headings is introduced, talk about what will go in that section. The following notes may be helpful:

Spelling rules In here you will put all the rules you learn. For example, when you want to use the plural of a word which

SPELLING AND PHONICS KS2

ends in 'y', you can put an 's' on the end if it has a vowel before the 'y' (holiday/holidays), but if it has a consonant before the 'y', you have to take off the 'y' and use 'ies' (baby/babies).

Ways of remembering spellings A good way to remember the 'die' in 'soldier' is to remember 'soldiers die', or for the 'pie' in 'piece' remember 'a piece of pie'.

Silent letters We have a lot of these in English, like the 'b' in 'lamb' or the 'h' in 'ghost'. This is where you will collect what you know about these.

Prefixes and suffixes These are parts of words which can be added to change the meaning. The prefix goes at the beginning of the word: for example, 'un'+'happy' = 'unhappy'. The suffix goes at the end of the word: for example, 'grace'+'ful' = 'graceful'. This is where you will make a note about different kinds of prefixes and suffixes.

Word families These are words that you can remember because they all go together, like 'fright, frightened, frightening' or 'help, helpful, helper, helped, helping'.

Words about spelling This is where you can make a note of all the words we use to talk about spellings, like some of those we have used today, such as 'plural' and 'singular'. Turn to the correct section in your books and put in these two words, with their definitions.

'Singular' means there is only one of something (a house, a school).

'Plural' means there is more than one of something (two houses, two schools).

Do not go into too much detail about these last four headings, but explain that they will be able to make notes on these as they meet new information about spellings.

Now return to the first single page of the booklet. Ask the children to write the word 'Contents' at the top of this page and then to write down the following list. These could be written on the chalkboard for the children to copy.

Contents

1. Alphabetical list of words (A–Z)
2. Spelling rules
3. Ways of remembering spellings – mnemonics
4. Silent letters
5. Prefixes and suffixes
6. Word families
7. Words about spelling
8. Notes/interesting things about words

The booklet is now ready for use. Entries should be made whenever the children encounter something new. Many opportunities are highlighted throughout the activities in this book.

Suggestion(s) for extension

This booklet will be made as a whole class activity. Some children will do this quite quickly, so they could be given the task of adding more entries in the 'Words about spelling' section, to include definitions of all the words used during the making of the booklet (consonant, vowel, prefix, suffix, alphabetical order, etc).

Suggestion(s) for support

Many children will find this task quite demanding, so for them it would be a good idea to split the activity into two or three sessions: If they complete the naming and titling of the booklet and labelling the alphabet pages in the first session, they could label the other sections as a second activity and put in the definitions (singular and plural) and complete the contents page in a third session.

Assessment opportunities

This is not really an activity which can provide assessment opportunities other than general observations of individual children's level of understanding of the terminology used. Individuals may offer examples of some of the terms used and may volunteer definitions; these should be noted as part of your assessment of the child's understanding/attitude/contribution and so on.

Opportunities for IT

Children could use an art or graphics package to design an interesting cover for their personal spelling books. The design could be printed out and used to form the cover of their personal spelling book.

Aspects of the English PoS covered

Writing – 2d.

Rhymes & homophones

bare

The National Curriculum in Key Stage 2 places a special emphasis on helping children find 'alternative ways of writing the same sound'. Rhyming poetry provides a pleasurable and meaningful context for this knowledge to develop. By looking at the written form of rhyming words, children rapidly discover that the same sound can be represented in several different ways. This knowledge can then be extended by helping the children to expand their repertoire of word and rhyme families.

Introducing children to homophones (words that sound the same but are spelled differently) is another important way of helping them to think about spelling patterns and the irregularities that can occur in those patterns.

Some of the activities test the children's existing knowledge of spelling through using techniques such as 'have a go', which encourages the child to try to spell the word as best he can. The child is asked to think about the word, say it, visualise it and then try to spell it on paper. Having written the word once, if the child is not satisfied he should try again. Most teachers recommend at least three tries. Before he tries again, he should look at the previous attempt and identify parts of the word that might be spelled correctly and then work on the part that he feels is incorrect. Some children will write all the correct letters of the word, but not necessarily in the right order. 'Have a go' provides the opportunity to look again and sort the word out.

SPELLING AND
PHONICS KS2

BARELY BEAR!

To enable children to develop an interest in homophones and use them in their writing.

†† *Whole class and pairs.*

🕓 *1 hour.*

Previous skills/knowledge needed

The children will be aware that rhyming words and words that sound very similar can be represented in a number of different ways when written down. Through their work on rhyme and by looking at word families, children will have discovered words that match exactly in sound but differ in spelling and meaning. They may have commented, for example, that 'see' sounds like 'sea'. It is possible that in discussions teachers will have focused not only on the variation in spelling of these words but also talked about the difference in their meaning. This may have led to an introduction to the term 'homophone'. The children will have begun to make personal or class collections of these words.

Key background information

Potentially the most fascinating and yet confusing paradox for children is that of the homophone. Here the complete sound of the word is exactly the same and yet it can have two – sometimes three – meanings. In spoken language this is not a problem for children, as the meaning of the word is conveyed by the context in which it occurs. However, in order to distinguish and clarify the meaning in writing, the word has to be represented in different ways. This can prove to be a puzzling task. The move from spoken to written language takes time for children to develop and this would appear to explain why children require plenty of practice at sorting out the differences in the spelling of homophones. What might appear at face value as careless spelling mistakes may in fact be a sign that the child is still developing and stabilising her understanding of homophones and how they work.

Preparation

In a previous session make a class book of illustrated homophones. Photocopy, enlarge and laminate the 'Humorous homophone story' on page 108. Make a word-processed list of all the pairs of homophones known to the class and photocopy these for the children to share in pairs. On the flip chart write a list of homophones that the children know. Set up a computer with a word-processing package for the children to use in the support activity. Make a blank book to contain the children's stories.

Resources needed

Class or individual collection of homophones, photocopiable sheet 108, A4 paper (rough and good quality), pencils, pens, colouring pencils, felt-tipped pens, dictionaries, poetry books, flip chart or chalkboard, thin card, glue, laminating materials, computer with word-processing package.

A humorous homophone story

Bernie the bear went to see the sea. Barely had the bear arrived when he went to buy two buckets and spades.

'Oh, that was a bit expensive,' said Bernie, holding his change in his paw. 'I feel quite poor now and I don't think I can buy an ice-cream.'

Just then, his friends Katie and Alice came by with their picnic box. 'What have you got in there?' asked the hungry Bernie.

'Just a pair of pears,' laughed the girls.

All three friends sat on a wooden bench. 'Would you like to share our pears?' asked Katie and Alice.

'I don't know,' said Bernie. 'Well... it would be rude to say no!'

What to do

Start the session by talking about the children's individual or class collection of homophones. Introduce or remind the children about the term 'homophone' and explain that in this lesson they will be working with homophones.

Ask the children, in pairs, to spend a few moments brainstorming any more homophones that they know. Discuss the results and add to the list of homophones on the flip chart. Next, explain to the children that they will be writing their own short illustrated 'humorous homophone stories' in which amusing events will happen because of the pairs of homophones used. Provide an example, either by writing your own 'humorous homophone story' or by using the story on photocopiable page 108.

Read the story together. Then ask the children, working in twos, to look for the pairs of homophones. How many can they find? Ask them to identify them. Underline each pair on the sheet and draw quick illustrations above some of the

words to provide clarification.

Explain to the children that their task now is to write their own 'humorous homophone stories'. First, distribute the word-processed homophone sheet to the pairs of children. Ask them to read through the sheet and select three or more pairs of homophones for their stories. They should rehearse their stories aloud and write rough notes on paper. Encourage the children to use their partner as a sounding-board for their ideas. As they work, check the progress of the stories and ask children to read promising examples aloud to the group. Then ask them to write down the final version of their story. To conclude, ask some of the children to read their stories aloud to the group.

Suggestion(s) for extension
Some children might enjoy rewriting the story, omitting some of the homophone words and substituting illustrations instead. They could make up their own stories, using pairs of homophones (for example, see/sea, be/bee, sale/sail).

Suggestion(s) for support
Using the class collection of homophones as a resource bank, ask the children to select three pairs of words. Check that they understand the meaning of their chosen homophones, write the words on the flip chart and quickly illustrate them. Using the most productive pair of homophones, provide the children with a 'story start'. Write this on the flip chart and ask the children what might happen next. Draw their attention to the remaining two pairs of words. Rehearse the complete story thoroughly with the group and then ask them to have a go at writing down their version. If some children still find this too difficult, ensure that the pairs of words selected for the story can be represented by drawings. Rehearse the story with the children and then ask them to draw a sequenced picture story. Then, if necessary, scribe their stories. If possible, the children should word-process the story and place the writing under the appropriate parts of the sequence. Alternatively, the story could be a collaborative piece of work, with the teacher scribing.

Assessment opportunities
The first stage of the main activity provides opportunities to judge the children's existing knowledge of homophones. This will provide guidance for the most appropriate method of following the activity through with each child. The demonstration story will provide the children with opportunities to identify the homophones and comment on their graphic differences. Writing independent stories successfully will be challenging and children's rough working should be monitored as well as the final draft. In the support activity, listen to the children's spoken version of their stories which will indicate their growing awareness of homophones.

Opportunities for IT
Working in pairs, the children could use a word processor to originate their 'humorous homophone story'. After printing out their first draft, they could work away from the computer to edit and redraft their original story. They could return to the computer to undertake final editing. In order to do this the children will need to save their work on a disk so that they can retrieve it at a later time.

Children could add illustrations to their story, either by drawing their own pictures using a graphics or art package, or select suitable pictures from clip art collections or CD-ROM images such as the SEMERC *Treasure Chest* CD-ROM. This will give children an opportunity to combine more than one type of media and to resize and position their graphics on the screen.

Display ideas
Having completed their stories, the children should make neat copies for display purposes and illustrate them. They may choose to put small illustrations above the homophones in order to convey their meaning. The 'humorous homophone stories' could be compiled into a book, with a decorative cover, which can be read at story time.

Aspects of the English PoS covered
Speaking and listening – 1a, c.
Reading – 2a, c.
Writing – 2b, d.

Reference to photocopiable sheet
Photocopiable sheet 108 is for use in the main activity. It will need to be enlarged so that the whole class can read it together.

 AN EXPLORATION OF RHYME & ALLITERATION

> *To provide children with experience of listening to rhyme and alliteration and to relate the sound patterns that they hear to the patterns of letters in print.*
>
> †† *Whole class, then pairs or individuals.*
>
> 🕐 *Total of 50 minutes: 15 minutes whole group; 25 minutes individual activity; 10 minutes whole group.*

Previous skills/knowledge needed

Children will need to be familiar with a selection of rhyming poetry, some of which they will know off by heart. They will have some phonic and graphic knowledge, though this will still be developing. In discussion it may be revealed that some children experience difficulty at times in detecting rhyme and alliteration in poetry.

Key background information

Sensitivity to rhyme and alliteration is well established in many young children long before they come to school and has been shown to be crucial in their later success in reading. Bradley and Bryant in *Children's Reading Problems* (Blackwell, 1985) found that in a group of older children who were experiencing difficulties in their reading, a lack of sensitivity to rhyme and alliteration was a significant factor. It is important, therefore, to identify children in Key Stage 2 who may need further experience of rhyme and alliteration and to provide activities which develop and sustain this sensitivity.

Preparation

Make enough A4 copies of sheet 109 for each child (or pairs). Photocopy sheet 110 for the support activity. Select other rhyming poems to read to the children.

Resources needed

Photocopiable sheets 109 and 110, flip chart or chalkboard, pens, pencils, colouring pencils, poetry books containing rhyming poetry, good quality writing paper.

What to do

Explain to the children that the focus of the first part of the session will be on words that rhyme. Ask them to try to explain what is meant by the word 'rhyme'. They may offer examples such as 'ice' and 'rice'. Note these on the flip chart. Ask the children to listen as you say a set of words, all of which rhyme except for one. Can they hear the 'odd one out'? An example might be 'hat, cat, dog, mat, bat'. Increase the complexity of the sets of words.

Next, ask the children to recite any rhyming poems that they know off by heart and then read the children a selection of favourite rhyming poetry. An example would be Spike Milligan's poem called 'The Lion' (*Milliganimals*, Puffin, 1971). On the first reading, the children will probably laugh at the

humour. Before embarking on a second reading, ask the children to listen carefully and see if they can remember all the rhyming words that they hear in the poem. List these on the flip chart. Then read the poem through with the children, asking them to point out all the rhyming words. Do these match up with the words that they have already identified? What do they notice about the spellings? Which part of the words change and which remain constant? Why do they think that two words that sound similar can be spelled differently? Can they think of some more words that belong to the 'bite' and 'right' word families? List these on the flip chart.

Go on to remind the children that not only do poems use words that rhyme, but some use 'alliterative' words to create special effects. See if anyone can explain what the word 'alliteration' means. Write the word on the flip chart. Ask the children to listen to a set of alliterative words. Can they spot the 'odd one out'? An example might be 'car, cat, bag, carrot, cake'. Repeat with similar sets of words as necessary.

Then ask whether anyone can think of a poem that has alliteration in it. Introduce Edward Lear's 'The Pelican Chorus' from *Owls and Pussycats* (OUP, 1993). It may be interesting for the children to know that Lear was one of the greatest exponents of the 'nonsense rhyme'. 'The Pelican Chorus' is an excellent example of this. First read the extract from the poem through (see opposite page).

SPELLING AND PHONICS KS2

The Pelican Chorus

King and Queen of the Pelicans we;
No other Birds so grand we see!
None but we have feet like fins!
With lovely leathery throats and chins!
Puffskin, Pluffskin, Pelican jee!
We think no Birds so happy as we!
Plumpskin, Ploshkin, Pelican jill!
We think so then, and we thought so still!

Gather the children's initial responses to the poem and then read it again, this time asking them to listen carefully for the rhyming words. They should try to remember as many of the rhyming words as they can. Write up all the rhyming words that they can remember. Then give out copies of the poem on photocopiable page 109. Read the poem through with the children. Ask them to identify the rhyming words. They should notice that these occur at the end of each line. Encourage the children to discuss similarities and differences in the pairs of rhyming words.

After this, focus the children's attention on the alliterative lines in the poem. Read some of the lines out, starting with the obviously alliterative phrases such as 'Ploffskin, Pluffskin, Pelican jee!' What sound can they hear at the beginning of the nonsense words? At a more challenging level ask, 'What sound can you hear in the middle of "Ploffskin" and "Pluffskin"?' Some children may respond with 'sk' and others may hear the word 'skin'. Then move on to more subtle examples of alliteration such as 'With lovely leathery throats and chins!' The 'th' sound in 'leathery' and 'throats' adds to the alliterative effect. The 'th' is also strongly in evidence in the last line. Draw the children's attention to the written form of the poem and ask them to identify lines which contain words starting with the same letter. Then see if they can find the more complex alliterative patterns described above.

Working individually (or if preferred in pairs) with their own copies of 'The Pelican Chorus' (photocopiable page 109), the children should then underline the rhyming words and identify some of the alliterative patterns. Finally, teach the whole group all or part of the verse, so that they can recite it off by heart.

Suggestion(s) for extension
Children who demonstrate a clear understanding of the activity could go on to write their own variations on the verse, substituting keywords such as 'Pelican' with another animal and changing the alliterative pattern of 'Ploffskin, Pluffskin' and 'Plumpskin, Ploshkin'. They should first rehearse their versions by reciting them to a partner and then amend their drafts. The finished poems should be written up neatly and illustrated.

Suggestion(s) for support
Children who have difficulty in identifying the rhymes and alliterative words could be given half of 'The Pelican Chorus' to work with. Their attention should be drawn to the final words in each line and they should be told which initial letters to look out for when looking for the alliterative patterns.

To enable these children to write their own version of the poem, photocopiable sheet 110 has been provided with some words left out. This is designed to enable the children to focus on specific words which can be changed. Rehearse

alternatives with the children first to help them. Alternatively, enlarge the sheet and work as a group to produce a shared writing poem.

Assessment opportunities

The 'odd one out' activity, which introduces both parts of the main activity, provides an opportunity to gain an initial impression of how well the children can hear rhyming and alliterative words. As they listen to the poems and look at the spelling of the rhyming words, children will reveal in their comments their growing awareness of similarities and differences within rhymes. With the alliterative words, they should comment on the initial consonants and other repetitive patterns within words. By writing their own versions of 'The Pelican Chorus' the children will show how far they can handle alternative rhymes and alliterative patterns.

Opportunities for IT

Children could use a word processor with a copy of the Pelican Chorus already prepared by the teacher and saved on a disk. The children could load the file into the word processor and substitute new alliterative words. It is important that they do not delete all of the text back to the word they wish to change and they will need to be shown how to move the cursor around the screen to the words to be altered and make deletions and insertions into the text. The final version could be saved and printed out for display purposes.

The children might also use the speech facility of a talking word processor to listen to the alliterative poems. Some children may notice that although they can speed up the speech it does not copy the rhythm of the poem. This would be a good time to discuss some of the limitations of the speech facility.

Display ideas

Make an enlarged poetry card of 'The Pelican Chorus' and surround it with the children's own alternative, illustrated versions of the poem.

Aspects of the English PoS covered

Speaking and listening – 1a.
Reading – 1a; 2a.
Writing – 1c; 2d.

Reference to photocopiable sheets

Photocopiable sheet 109 is a copy of the poem that will be needed for the main activity. Photocopiable sheet 110 has been designed specifically to help those children who need support.

THE ILLUSTRATED HOMOPHONE HANDBOOK

To develop children's understanding of homophones.
Whole class and pairs.
45 minutes.

Previous skills/knowledge needed

Through their reading and writing of rhyming poetry, children will have become aware that sounds can be represented in a number of ways when written down. By building families of monosyllabic rhyming words, they may have listed words that sound exactly the same but are spelled differently – for example, 'been' and 'bean'. These discussions are likely to have centred not only on the spelling but also on the meaning of the word. The children may have been introduced to the term 'homophone'.

Key background information

The English language contains many paradoxes, such as the inconsistent relationship between some spoken sounds and their written symbols. The analysis of rhyming words will further reveal these paradoxes by demonstrating to children that the same rhyming sound can be represented in several different ways in its written form.

As stated in the activity 'Barely Bear!' the move from spoken to written language can take time for some children. For example, they have to learn to make their meanings much more explicit when they express an idea in writing. The transposition of the spoken language to the written form can clearly be seen when they need to decide on which homophone to use. Sometimes children master one way of spelling the word and use this spelling in an arbitrary way to serve all purposes and meanings. Other children are aware of and use both spellings but become unsure as to which to use in their writing.

SPELLING AND PHONICS KS2

Some teachers believe that looking at the spelling of the homophones together simply adds to the confusion, yet children will meet the words in their reading and will need to use them in their writing. Therefore addressing the paradox seems to be a positive way forward in Key Stage 2.

Preparation

Make a book with more pages than there are children in the class and cover it with thick card. Cut the good quality paper slightly smaller than the pages in the book. Set up the word-processing package on the computer. Set up a cassette recorder with a blank tape. From a rhyming poem select a verse which contains a rhyme that can be used as the basis of a rhyme family. Ensure that this family will produce some homophones: for example, words that rhyme with 'Spain' could include 'main' and 'mane', 'reign' and 'rain'. Type out the verse, enlarge it on the photocopier and mount on to A3 card to use as a poetry card. An example of a suitable poem is this extract from *Curtis the Hip-Hop Cat* by Gini Wade (Macmillan Children's Books, 1986).

> Then Curtis showed all his friends at school
> The other kits thought, 'Breakdancing's cool!'
> Now this new dance craze has hit the street
> Everybody's looking for the Purrfect Beat.
>
> Now this is the story of Hip-Hop cat
> Get down, Curtis, and burn up the mat!

Resources needed

Materials to make an A4 blank book, sheets of good quality paper, rulers, glue, writing materials, erasers, crayons or felt-tipped pens, flip chart or chalkboard, dictionaries, rough paper, computer with a word-processing program, printer, rhyming poetry book, A3 card, cassette recorder with blank cassette and headphones for the support activity.

What to do

With the whole group together, read your selected poem to them. Then reread a carefully selected verse (see 'Preparation'). Display the poetry card so that it is visible to the whole group.

Next, ask the group to identify the rhymes. Focus on the rhyme that will produce homophones and ask the class to brainstorm a list of all the possible rhyming words. List the rhymes on the flip chart, for example 'beat, street, heat, sheet, fleet, neat, meat, meet, seat'.

If a child suggests one of the possible homophone words, *before* writing it ask him to clarify which meaning of the word he was thinking of. This will indicate to the class the need to distinguish meaning in order to decide how the word will be spelled (an important point that they need to grasp in order to make the transition between spoken and written homophones). Ask the child to suggest the spelling. Then ask the group what the other meaning of the word might be and how that might be spelled. Write this down also. At this point leave the rhyming list of words and shift the focus on to the homophones by asking the children if they know the special name that is given to words that sound exactly the same but are spelled differently. If they do not know, introduce the term 'homophone' and write it on the flip chart.

Explain to the children that their focus in the session is going to be on homophones. They are going to make a collection of homophones to put into a special class reference book called 'The Homophone Handbook'. Show the class the ready-made book. Explain that the book is intended to help them with their writing: they can use it to check which spelling of the homophones they need. Pairs of homophones will be written in the book and illustrated with pictures so that each picture clearly conveys the meaning of the word it represents. Although the book is not an alphabet book, the pairs of homophones will be put in the book in alphabetical order so that they are easier to locate.

For the first five minutes ask the children to work in pairs and to note down on rough paper any pairs of homophones that they already know. When they are ready, ask them to read their lists aloud and collect their homophones into one list on the flip chart. There will be some overlap, so remind the children to read out only those pairs that have not already been suggested. As they feed back their list, agree with each pair which homophone they will be working on (see the support activity for allocation of words). Discuss spellings as the need arises and check that the children are clear about the meanings.

Using one pair of homophones, provide a demonstration on the flip chart of how each word can be illustrated and defined through its illustration. For example, 'there' might be represented by a person showing someone else which direction to go in; one of the figures could be pointing to a building in the distance or a road. 'Their' could be represented by a group of children stroking a pet or holding an object.

Talk about definitions, using a dictionary to demonstrate the meaning of each term. Ask the children to help by offering a verbal definition based on what the illustration is saying to them.

Working in pairs, the children should now discuss their homophones and decide who will concentrate on which word. They should use rough paper first to try out their illustration and should consult their partners, to see if they are communicating the meaning effectively. Some of the more abstract words such as 'been' and 'too' will require careful thought and the sharing of ideas. When the children are satisfied with their rough drawings, they should work on the final version. They should then check the spelling of their word, type it on the computer, print it out and cut it to size, ready to stick on to the illustration. Once the homophones are completed, they should be sorted into alphabetical sequence before being stuck into 'The Homophone Handbook'. It is advisable to halt the activity periodically to check on progress, to share examples that are working well and to offer help to those who are having difficulty expressing their ideas.

children are working with concrete, rather than abstract, words, such as 'hair' and 'hare'. It may help the children to rehearse the meaning of the words by saying their ideas aloud first. You could ask a question about the word or pose a riddle. (For example, 'You brush it with a hairbrush'; answer: hair.) This should give the child a clearer image of what she could draw. The same approach may help the child to prepare the written definition of her word; the question can be converted into a statement.

Further support can be provided by making a tape called the 'homophone quiz tape' in which a simple riddle is asked about some of the easier words. For example, 'You can eat it. It tastes nice in tomato sauce.' (Answer: bean.) The supplementary question – 'Can you spell the word bean?' – will draw attention to the differences in spelling between the homophones. A further example might be: 'It falls from the sky and makes you wet.' (Answer: rain.) 'Can you spell rain?'

Suggestion(s) for extension

On rough paper the children can work on drafting a written definition of each homophone. They should seek feedback from their partners and then refer to a dictionary to see how well they have managed to express their ideas. Once they are satisfied with the definition, they can type it on the word processor and stick it in 'The Homophone Handbook' to accompany the illustration. It is important that the children do not simply go straight to the dictionary and copy out a definition. They need to reflect on the meanings of the pairs of words, especially if they are going to be able to differentiate between them in the future. Copying does not necessarily lead to this level of reflection. Sometimes dictionary definitions are too concise for the children to understand fully the meaning of a word.

Suggestion(s) for support

Some children will find the main activity too demanding. They may find it difficult to produce a meaningful illustration. When the homophone pairings are allocated, ensure that these

Assessment opportunities

Children who can volunteer homophones during the brainstorming session will demonstrate their existing awareness. Some children will have an extensive bank of homophones which they have already 'collected' and may be demonstrating this knowledge in their written work. This will be further revealed in the definitions they write for the class book. For some children, focusing on the different meanings of the words will be an important experience, requiring plenty of further practice. Asking riddles and posing questions will help develop their ability to distinguish between homophones. After the book has been completed, it will be interesting to see which children actively consult it in order to clarify uncertainties about spelling.

It will be useful to look through a range of the children's independent writing to monitor their use of homophones and to draw their attention to any confusion. Encourage these children to talk about the intended meaning of the word in their written work and then ask them to consult 'The Homophone Handbook' to double-check their definition. Note which children are using the term 'homophone'.

Opportunities for IT

An alternative approach would be to set up a word processor desktop publishing package with a separate page for each

child or pair of children. The children could then type in their homophone pair and select a suitable font and size to display the words on their page. They could also add their own written definitions to the pair of words, possibly using a computer thesaurus for assistance. This page could then be printed out and children could hand-draw their illustration. The pages could be placed into transparent sleeves in a ring-binder to make a book.

The children could also use an art or graphics package to design their own pictures on the computer. As this is likely to be a different piece of software, they will need to be shown how to transfer their picture on to the word processor page. This may involve them in saving their picture on a disk and then inserting it into the word processor using computer or software specific functions. If children found the illustrations difficult to draw on the computer, they might be able to use pictures from collections of clip art or CD-ROMs.

Another approach to the illustrations would be to scan children's hand-drawn illustrations and use the digitised picture by placing it in the homophone pair page. Black and white illustrations could be coloured in by hand after they have been printed out.

These approaches would enable pupils to achieve some of the higher levels of IT capability by integrating various forms of media for a presentation to an audience.

Display ideas

Ask one pair of children to write the title on the front cover of 'The Homophone Handbook' and to illustrate it. The book can be added to as the class think of more pairs of words. The children should refer to the book when they are proofreading their writing, especially if they know that they find certain words confusing.

The 'homophone quiz tape' can be made available and the children provided with answer sheets on which to write down their solutions to the riddles. The children can also add new riddles and questions to the tape. The tape may be helpful when children are trying to clarify the meanings of homophones.

Aspects of the English PoS covered

Speaking and listening – 1a.
Reading – 2a, c.
Writing – 2d.

EXPLORING SPELLING FAMILIES

To help children recognise that there are alternative ways of spelling the same sound and to analyse what some of these alternatives might be through the use of appropriate terminology. To introduce the term 'homophone'.

†† *Whole class, then pairs. Also suitable for small group activity.*

🕐 *1 hour.*

Previous skills/knowledge needed

The children will have had considerable experience of hearing a wide range of rhyming poetry and also of writing rhyming poetry. They will have noticed, particularly when writing, that although words that rhyme sound similar their written forms may differ. Some children may have realised that within one rhyme family there may be several spelling families. The children will have had some experience of using the terms 'vowel' and 'consonant'. They will have discussed some of these issues and shown their understanding orally in class.

Key background information

Many sounds follow regular phonic patterns. However, the spelling system also has a sizeable minority of words that contain inconsistencies. Some of these inconsistencies have occurred for historical reasons, others because the limited number of symbols in the alphabet have to represent a much greater number of spoken sounds. It is helpful, therefore, to encourage children's curiosity about the alternative ways of representing sounds in written language. By looking at written rhymes, children are able to focus on the similarities and differences. In order to do this effectively, they must be equipped with appropriate terminology ('vowel' and 'consonant') which will enable them to discuss words analytically.

Preparation

Select poems which demonstrate how words can rhyme but follow different spelling patterns. An example is *My Cat Likes to Hide in Boxes* by Eve Sutton and Lynley Dodd (Puffin,

SPELLING AND PHONICS KS2

1978), an extract from which is provided below. This can be typed out and enlarged on the photocopier before being mounted on A3 card. Make a list of all the possible words that rhyme with those to be discussed. Choose one pair of rhymes to focus on in depth (see the example of 'Spain' and 'aeroplane' in 'What to do'). Make a word-processed list of all the possible words that will rhyme with the pair of words and photocopy it for the children to use in pairs. (If working with the extract from 'My Cat Likes to Hide in Boxes', use photocopiable sheet 111.) Cut a sheet of thin A4 card into 16 equal pieces for use with the support activity. Use a contrasting sheet of A3 paper to mount the pieces of card on. Select verses with more complex rhymes, word-process and photocopy them for use in the extension activity.

Resources needed

Rhyming poetry books, flip chart or chalkboard, felt-tipped pens, A4 paper, rulers, writing materials, dictionaries, one sheet of thin A3 card, glue, scissors, photocopiable sheets 111 and 112, one sheet of thin A4 card and sheet of A3 paper for support activity, rough paper.

What to do

Start off by reading some rhyming poetry to the whole class and asking them to share any rhyming poems that they know. Place the enlarged poetry card on the flip chart and read the verse.

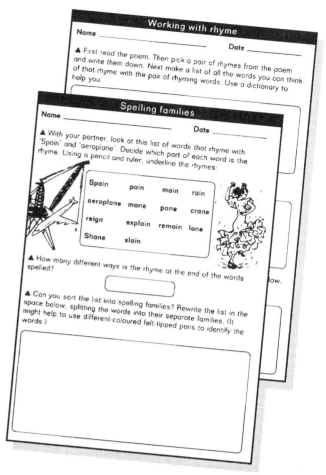

My Cat Likes to Hide in Boxes

The cat from Greece
Joined the police.
The cat from Norway
Got stuck in the doorway.
The cat from Spain
Flew an aeroplane.
The cat from France
Liked to sing and dance,
But MY cat likes to hide in boxes.

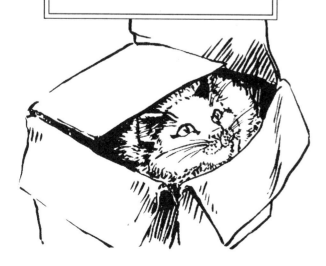

Ask the children to identify the pairs of rhymes. Then ask them to look more closely at the spelling of the rhyming pairs. What do they notice? They should comment that 'France' and 'dance' have the same rhyming spelling but the other pairs do not. Select the most productive pair of words in terms of generating new rhymes (which in this case is probably 'Spain' and 'aeroplane'). Write the words on the flip chart or chalkboard and ask the children to think of some more words that rhyme with them. Write down all the suggestions. The list might look like this: Spain, aeroplane, pain, main, mane, pane, slain, rain, Shane, crane, explain, remain, lane, reign. Now read the list through with the group and ask them to identify the sound of the rhyme.

Next, give out the photocopied bank of rhyming words (sheet 111 or your own list) and ask the children, working in pairs, to identify which part of each of the words is the rhyme. They should underline the rhyming parts. Allow five minutes for this and then ask each pair to underline one of the rhymes on the main chart as they have done on their photocopied sheet.

Now ask the children, still working in pairs, to look at the list again in order to see how many different ways the rhyme is spelled. Can they sort the words out into different spelling families? They can either use different coloured felt-tipped pens to code the words or rewrite them in separate lists on the photocopiable sheet. Allow up to 15 minutes for this and

then summarise the children's findings on the flip chart or chalkboard by writing the words in their spelling groups.

Tell the children that they have proved that the same sound can be spelled in several different ways. In the example on the worksheet the focus of discussion should be on the vowel digraphs 'ai' and 'ei' and the long vowel 'a' in the words, as well as the role of silent 'e'. The children should also notice that the stable letter in all the words is the consonant 'n'. (So that the children can talk analytically about the structure of the words, essential terminology should be introduced and used.) In this particular example, three ways of representing the sound have been found. It is important for the children to realise that when they are writing, if they are unsure of how a word might be spelled, they should consider the possible options by thinking about the spelling families.

To conclude, ask the children if they have noticed something else that is interesting about some of the words. The intention here is that someone will notice the pairs of words that are homophones (words that sound exactly the same but are spelled differently and have different meanings). They should identify 'rain' and 'reign', 'pain' and 'pane'. Introduce the term 'homophone' and explain its meaning. Can they think of some more pairs of words that sound the same but are spelled differently? List these words on the flip chart or chalkboard.

Suggestion(s) for extension

Provide photocopies of a more challenging extract of rhyming poetry. There are useful examples in: *Song of the City* by Gareth Owen (Armada Books, 1985), *Heard it in the Playground* by Allan Ahlberg (Puffin, 1991), *Classic Poems to Read Aloud* selected by James Berry (Kingfisher, 1995). Ask the children to look at the rhymes and identify a pair to explore. Using photocopiable sheet 112, they should follow the procedure in the main activity by first of all listing all the possible rhyming words they can think of (they can use dictionaries to help them). They should then separate the list into spelling families. Finally, they should make a list of any homophones that have occurred during the activity.

Suggestion(s) for support

Using a familiar rhyming poem, help the children to select a pair of rhyming words to study. Each child should then suggest all the words he can think of that rhyme with the pair of words. Write these down on a piece of rough paper for the child and then ask him to read the set of words. Next, using a fine felt-tipped pen, he should copy each word on to a piece of card (see 'Preparation'). Once this stage is completed, the child can then sort the words more easily into spelling families. The cards could then be carefully mounted on to a sheet of contrasting-coloured A3 paper and an explanatory statement written. The heading might read 'I have found ___ ways of spelling words that rhyme with ___'.

Assessment opportunities

During the main activity the children will reveal whether or not they can identify words that sound the same. When using the enlarged poetry card, the children may rapidly draw attention to the graphic differences in the words. It is likely that these children will also successfully sort the list of rhyming words into spelling families. Working independently with their own pairs of rhymes, they are likely to demonstrate this confidence again. Encouraging the children to discuss the differences and commonalties in the structure of words will make explicit their growing awareness of the spelling system. Note which children successfully employ terminology such as 'vowel' and 'consonant' to help them in this.

Some children will identify the homophones in the rhyming list and may demonstrate that they can use the term 'homophone' appropriately. The children may be able to distinguish between the different meanings of words that are homophones. They may be able to generate a further list of homophones.

Children experiencing serious difficulties may have problems in building a set of rhyming words. This may be due to a lack of sensitivity to rhyme and may indicate the need for a lot more experience of listening to rhyming poetry. Their attention should be drawn to the words that rhyme.

Opportunities for IT

Children could use a word processor or simple desktop publishing package to present their lists for classroom display. If a word processor is used, the children will need to be taught how to set and use the Tab function in order to create vertical lists without using the space bar to position words on the screen. If a desktop publishing package is used, separate frames can be set up for different lists.

For example:

▲ Using the word processor

Spain (press Tab)	plane (press Tab)	reign
pain (press Tab)	etc	

▲ Using the DTP package

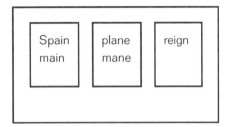

Display ideas

Children working on the extension activity can present their findings in a form suitable for display. A possible title might be 'All you ever wanted to know about the ____, ____ and ____ sound'. The children working on the support activity will produce a finished product for display purposes. Write an overall heading for the display – 'Words that have the same rhyme can be spelled in several different ways'. Set up a class list of pairs of homophones, which the children can add to as they come across them.

Aspects of the English PoS covered

Reading – 2a.
Writing – 2a, d, e.

Reference to photocopiable sheets

Photocopiable sheet 111 should be used in conjunction with the extract from 'My Cat Likes to Hide in Boxes'. Photocopiable sheet 112 can be used with whatever extract of rhyming poetry is chosen for the extension activity.

RHYMING 'DOGGEREL'

To focus on rhymes and the different spellings of homophones.

†† *Whole class, then groups or pairs, then whole class to conclude.*

🕐 *Total of 1 hour: 15 minutes introduction; 20–30 minutes writing; 15–20 minutes conclusion.*

Previous skills/knowledge needed

The children will need to have had some experience of hearing rhyming poetry and of picking out pairs of rhyming words.

Key background information

The activity is intended to develop children's existing 'phonological awareness' and sensitivity to rhyme, which are important factors in their success in learning to read. At Key Stage 2 there will still be some children whose sensitivity in these areas needs to be developed further. This activity aims to extend their awareness into looking for ways of creating the same sound by using different letters, so it will be valuable also for children whose awareness of sounds is well developed, but who may not have become aware of particular letter patterns and the way in which these are used in spelling words.

Preparation

Make a copy of 'Down behind the dustbin' from Michael Rosen's *You Can't Catch Me*, (Deutsch, 1981) on a large sheet of paper (at least A3 size) for use with the whole group. The verse is as follows:

Down behind the dustbin
I met a dog called Sid.
He said he didn't know me
But I'm pretty sure he did.

A book with blank pages should be made for the children's completed verses. There should be at least as many pages as there are children in the class. The book should be made with A2 or A3 size paper, folded at the centre, with a cover of a different colour. The pages should be stitched along the fold, rather than stapled, because of the number of pages needed and the amount of use the book is likely to have.

Resources needed

Copy of the poem (see 'Preparation'), flip chart and large felt-tipped pens (or chalkboard and chalk), rough paper and pencils for first drafts, good quality paper (A4), pens, line-guides and paper-clips if using plain paper, handwriting pens for final copy, made-up book (see 'Preparation').

What to do

Begin the session by reading one or two rhyming poems from the book *You Can't Catch Me* (Deutsch, 1981) or another collection of Michael Rosen's poems. Tell the children to listen out for rhymes and after the reading ask which they can remember. Write the words on the flip chart or chalkboard and point out the letter strings in the rhyming pairs.

Next, place the copy of 'Down behind the dustbin' where all children can see it and read it together. Point out the rhymes and their spelling. Ask the children to make up a different version of the poem, keeping to the same pattern. One group of children came up with the following verses:

> Down behind the dustbin
> I met a dog called Mike.
> I said, 'What are young doing there?'
> 'I'm riding a bike.'
>
> Down behind the dustbin
> I met a dog called Nelly.
> I said, 'What are you doing there?'
> 'I'm playing with some jelly.'

These offered useful opportunities to look at rhymes with the same letter patterns, while a third offering enabled the teacher to point out the different spelling of the same sound:

> Down behind the dustbin
> I met a dog called Bear
> Who looked very sad
> 'Cos he fell off a chair.

Sometimes children will choose half-rhymes such as 'Sam' and 'van', 'Bill' and 'meal', or 'Wales' and 'shells'. These provide further opportunities to discuss where the half-rhyme lies in each of the words and, again, the chance to focus on letter strings.

After the children have composed two or three verses collaboratively, they should be divided into small groups or pairs to go off and work on further verses. Each pair or group should be asked to provide up to three verses, written on rough paper. When they have done this, ask them to list the pairs of rhymes on a separate sheet of paper, then to decide whether the rhymes use the same letter pattern or a different one and to write 'Same' or 'Different' beside each pair. When all the children have written at least some verses and have looked at their rhymes, bring the group back together and ask each pair or group to read out their pairs of rhymes. As the children do this write the words on the flip chart or chalkboard, placed in columns of the same *sound* (half-rhymes should be written in brackets). For example:

Bear	Sam	Patch	Bill
chair	(van)	catch	ill
Clare	Tam	(Butch)	Jill
hair	scram	(watch)	pill

The children should notice that some sounds can be spelled in more than one way, while others, usually the shorter words, can be spelled in only one way. Similarly, they may comment on the different pronunciation of the same letter strings (such as watched/catch). If the children do not notice these things, then point them out.

After this discussion give each pair or group a particular letter string and ask them to collect as many words as they can which have those letters in them. This is an ongoing activity which could continue for several days, or even weeks! Some of these lists could be very long, so several pairs or groups could collect the same letter patterns and combine them as a follow-up activity.

At this stage the children should also write out their edited verses on good quality paper, illustrate them and then stick them into the ready-made book. This final activity should be viewed as an opportunity for practice of their best handwriting, preferably using pens (see 'Display ideas').

Suggestion(s) for extension

Children who have been able to compose new verses for the poem without any difficulty could be encouraged to choose another verse with a form which they could adapt, and write new verses for this. If a group of children wished to work together they could look at some ballads – such as those in *A World of Poetry* selected by Michael Rosen (Kingfisher, 1995). The ballad form is not difficult to use, and

they could be encouraged to try writing a 'Ballad of...', as a collaboration within the group.

As a development of the spelling activity, they could be asked to collect words with the least common letter patterns in them, trying to find as many homophones as possible (for example, sight/site, right/write).

Suggestion(s) for support

Children who find composing the verses more difficult should work alongside those who find the task easier. When collecting words with the same letter patterns, the focus should be on those patterns which the teacher has observed they need to learn.

Assessment opportunities

During the discussion you will be able to observe which children show awareness of rhymes, including sensitivity to half-rhymes, as well as their knowledge of particular letter patterns. Make a note of such observations, so that you can plan further activities to develop individuals' knowledge.

Opportunities for IT

Children could use a word processor to originate their rhyming doggerel using the computer rather than just using the IT to present previously written work. Although the rhyming doggerel is a fairly short section of text to be entered, this activity will need to be spread over several days to give each child enough computer time. To speed up the process children could work at the computer on their first attempt, save it on a disk and then print it out to redraft away from the computer, allowing another child to work at the computer. The first child could then return to retrieve her first version from the disk and edit it. If the school has access to laptop computers this would speed up the writing process by allowing more children to write at the same time.

The final versions could be printed out in a suitable font style and size and the pages stuck on to the prepared book. An alternative approach to the book would be to place each page in a transparent sleeve and insert in a ring-binder.

Display ideas

The book of 'Down behind the dustbin' rhymes should be displayed where it is accessible for children to read to each other. Texts composed by the children in this way make very appealing reading matter, especially for those who do not read confidently. The fact that the rhyme has a very repetitive pattern and that the children will be familiar with many of the words will make the reading easier and help to promote confidence in the least fluent readers.

Aspects of the English PoS covered

Writing – 2d.
Speaking and listening – 1a.
Reading – 2a.

WRITING LIMERICKS: THE SPELLING OF SOUNDS

To raise children's awareness that there are alternative ways of spelling the same sound. To develop this awareness through discussion and oral presentation.
†† *Whole class working as individuals, then in pairs.*
⏱ *Total of 1 hour: 35 minutes main activity; 15 minutes in pairs; 10 minutes whole group.*

Previous skills/knowledge needed

The children will need to have had a wide range of rhyming poetry read to them, including limericks. They may be able to recite some limericks off by heart. They will have had some experience of writing rhyming poetry and may have noticed that although many words have similar rhymes, the written form of the rhymes is not necessarily the same.

Key background information

Although many words follow regular phonic patterns, the spelling system also contains inconsistencies. These inconsistencies have occurred partly because the 26 letters of the alphabet have to represent the 44-plus sounds in the spoken form of the language. There are also historical reasons, because English is a living language that is susceptible to change. It is important, therefore, to help children recognise that there are often alternative ways of writing the sounds they hear in words and that this is an

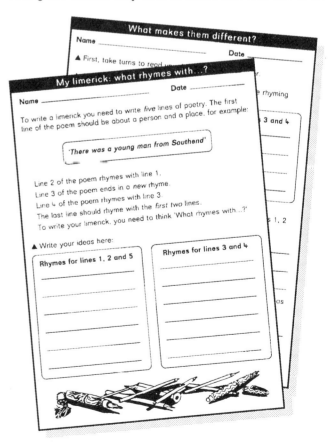

SPELLING AND
PHONICS KS2

interesting area to explore. The writing of rhyming poetry is an ideal medium for this kind of exploration.

The use of a highly structured form such as the limerick guarantees that these inconsistencies will be revealed. A typical limerick consists of a single stanza of five lines: the first two lines have three feet, the third and fourth two feet, and the final line returns to three feet. The usual rhyme scheme of a limerick is based on two rhymes: AABBA. It is this tight rhyme pattern that causes the inconsistencies to appear. The main purpose of this activity is for the children to talk about their findings.

Preparation
For your own reference select some limericks, or use the examples below from Iona and Peter Opie, eds., *The Oxford Dictionary of Nursery Rhymes*, (Oxford University Press, 1992). These are from the first known book of limericks, *The History of Sixteen Wonderful Old Women* (J. Harris, 1820, reprinted in Opie, I. and P., eds., 1992).

The Old Woman of Norwich
There was an old woman of Norwich,
Who lived upon nothing but porridge;
Parading the town,
She turned cloak into gown,
The thrifty old woman of Norwich.

The Old Woman of Surrey
There was an old woman of Surrey,
Who was morn, noon and night in a hurry;
Called her husband a fool,
Drove her children to school,
The worrying old woman of Surrey.

Using A4 paper, word-process one of the limericks and make an enlarged copy of it. Mount it on A3 card to use with the whole class. Make enough copies of photocopiable sheet 113 (one for each child) and photocopiable sheet 114 (one per pair).

Resources needed
Books of limericks, such as Edward Lear's *Nonsense Rhyme* (Ladybird, 1995), or Edward Lear's *A Book of Bosh* (Puffin, 1986), photocopiable sheets 113 and 114, pencils, pens, drawing materials, A3 card, glue, dictionaries, alphabet books, flip chart or chalkboard, cassette recorder with blank tape and headphones for the support activity.

What to do
Start off by reading the children a limerick (see 'Preparation'). Ask if they can identify what kind of poem it is. How do they know this is a limerick? Do they know some more limericks? Let the children recite theirs. Ask them what special features a limerick has. Use the enlarged limerick card to help the children make the key points about line and rhyme structure (see 'Key background information'). Encourage the children to talk about the irregularities in the spelling patterns of some of the rhyming words. To help them get a feel of the rhyme, recite a limerick together and clap and count the pattern.

Tell the children that they are going to write their own limerick. Remind the class that limericks usually start with a person who lives somewhere and give some examples. Brainstorm some possible opening lines and write them on the flip chart or chalkboard. Tell them that usually in a limerick something amusing or unfortunate happens to the person. Check that they understand the rhyming pattern. This should make their task easier as they only have to concentrate on thinking of two sets of rhyming words. Show the children the 'My limerick: what rhymes with...?' sheet on page 113 that they will be using to help them collect and try out possible rhymes for their limerick.

Ask the children to try to write their limerick. They may find that it helps to say the poem aloud to themselves as they compose. After they have written their first line, the children should now use photocopiable sheet 113. The name at the end of the first line will provide one of the rhymes. Encourage the children to use the class dictionaries to help them in their search for words and spellings.

After 15 minutes or so, ask the children to pair up with a response partner (someone that they are used to working with) for 15 minutes. Explain that the response partner's role is first to listen to and appreciate their limerick and then to look carefully at the rhymes and their spellings. Using the 'What makes them different?' sheet on page 114 (one between two), the children should look at one rhyme from each limerick and analyse the differences in the spellings. These differences should be recorded in note form. For the

final ten minutes of the session call the whole group back together and ask the pairs to share some of the differences that they found. List these on the flip chart and help the children understand the fact that certain sounds can be represented differently in writing.

Suggestion(s) for extension

Working from their findings noted on the 'What makes them different?' sheet, ask each pair to take one of the rhymes and make a list of all the words they can think of that rhyme with the word they have chosen. They should use dictionaries to help them. Having made their list and checked any doubtful spellings, they should then try to identify the separate spelling families that are present in their list. The children could then prepare a short presentation to the whole group in which they talk about some of their discoveries. They may notice that some words which sound the same are spelled differently. This will provide an opportunity to introduce the term 'homophone'.

Suggestion(s) for support

Some children will benefit from a collaborative session where they compose a limerick in a small group, with the teacher writing on the flip chart. They may find it easier to rehearse their limerick on the cassette recorder and listen to it before they try to write it down. Listen to their rhyme with them and make a word bank of essential words that they might need help with. Draw their attention to the rhyming words and encourage them to talk about similarities and differences. Take one of the rhyming words and list a family of words that sound the same. Look at the list and talk about words that belong in different spelling families. Can the children spot the differences? Each child should present one fact that she has found out to the whole group.

Assessment opportunities

When reading the limerick card, the children should comment on differences in the graphic representation of the same or similar sounds. When they analyse the rhyme structure of their own limericks and present their findings they should also comment on the fact that words can share similar sounds but the sounds can be spelled in different ways. The extension activity provides an opportunity to present their analysis of the possible ways of representing a sound.

By listening to what the children say it will be possible to gauge their current level of understanding. In the class discussion some children may look at the spelling families and think of more alternatives. Finally, some children will comment on homophones. Some may use the term to describe words that sound the same and are spelled differently. When talking about the spelling of the words, children may use the terms 'consonant' and 'vowel'.

Opportunities for IT

Children could use a word processor to originate their limericks at the keyboard rather than using the IT solely to present work that has already been written. Although the limerick will be a fairly short section of text to be entered this activity will probably need to be spread over several days to give each child enough computer time. To speed up the process children could work on their first attempt, save it on a disk and then print it out to redraft away from the computer, allowing another child to be working at the computer. The first child could then return to retrieve his first version from the disk and edit it. If the school has access to laptop computers this would speed up the writing process by allowing more children to write at the same time. The final versions could be printed out in a suitable font style and size for classroom display or bound together to make a class book of limericks.

Display ideas

The limericks could be illustrated and collected into a book. They could also be recorded on tape to make an audio book. Children working on the extension activity could write out their findings, showing the different ways they have found of representing one sound. The title could be 'What we found out about the _____ sound'.

Aspects of the English PoS covered

Speaking and listening – 1a.
Reading – 2a.
Writing – 2a, d, e.

Reference to photocopiable sheets

Photocopiable sheets 113 and 114 will help the children focus on rhyming words and the different spellings of certain sounds.

💻 THE OLD JOKE BOOK

To use children's love of jokes and puns to look at words which sound the same, but have different meanings or spellings (homophones).

†† *Whole class for introduction, then individuals or groups/pairs, as the children choose.*

🕐 *15–20 minutes for introduction: periods of 15–20 minutes whenever the activity is continued by groups or individuals.*

Previous skills/knowledge needed

The children will need to have some familiarity with jokes and puns.

Key background information

Most children know and enjoy a great many jokes; this is a part of their natural interest in language and what it can do. Children's ability to play with language and their interest in doing so begins at a very early age. Long before they come to school, young children experiment with sounds and meanings and derive great pleasure from doing so. Evidence collected by people like Kornei Chukovsky (from *Two to Five*, University of California, 1971) and Iona and Peter Opie (*Children's Games in Street and Playground*, OUP, 1984; *The Singing Game*, OUP, 1988) and the existence of nonsense rhymes and nursery rhymes, shows the rich variety of children's language play. This activity aims to draw on this enthusiasm to show children what jokes do with language and how they work. Learning about meaning and spelling of words will be largely incidental, but it provides a context for reflection on words. An added bonus is that the jokes are short and thus provide accessible and interesting reading material for the less fluent readers.

Preparation

Ask the children to bring in any books of jokes they have and from these, along with any others from the class/school library, select jokes which use wordplay or homophones. Prepare a blank book from A3 paper, folded to make 20 or 40 A4 pages (depending on how long you want the collection to continue), with a cover of either lightweight card or paper of a different colour, and either stapled or stitched along the fold. Make copies of sheets 115 and 116 if required.

Resources needed

Class book (see 'Preparation'), rough notebooks, pencils, pens, as wide a selection as possible of joke books, photocopiable sheets 115 and 116.

What to do

Begin by asking the children if they know any *short* jokes. (Short ones are more likely to play with words

and meanings.) Allow a few children to tell some jokes, listening out for those of the type you need, for example:

Question: What is the difference between a sheep and a dog?

Answer: One carries the fleece, while the other carries the fleas.

Question: When do bees have plenty of money?

Answer: When they sell (cell) their honey.

If none of this kind is offered, read some you have selected from the joke books or use the starter sheets (pages 115 and 116). Ask the children to explain the jokes. Most children will be able to offer some explanation of the play on words, for example in 'fleece' and 'fleas', and 'sell' and 'cell'. Point out the similarities in sound and the differences in meaning and spelling of the words that are used.

When you feel that the children have understood what kind of jokes they are looking for, allow groups of them to start making a note of any jokes of this kind that they already know or to look through the joke books to find some, or provide copies of photocopiable sheets 115 and 116. Some 'Knock, knock' jokes fall into this category. The children should make a note of these in their rough notebooks and try to explain the meanings of the jokey words. This will be all that is needed to initiate the activity.

On subsequent days, allow different groups of children time during the day to continue the search and to make a

**SPELLING AND
PHONICS KS2**

note of jokes they find. After several sessions, check through their notes, get the children to edit their collection and let some of them write out the jokes in the prepared class joke book. Children may need a reminder from time to time that they are looking particularly for short jokes which play with words.

When a number of jokes have been recorded in the book, spend a further session sharing the jokes and talk about the words, their meanings and their spellings. Allow the collection to proceed as long as the children are interested.

Suggestion(s) for extension

For children who are confident in recognising the use of words in jokes, provide a list of homophones and ask them to try to make up jokes using the homophones. Explain what homophones are and how the term is constructed from the Greek words – 'homo', meaning 'the same', and 'phone', meaning 'sound', as in telephone. Successful jokes can be added to the class book.

Suggestion(s) for support

Some children will find this activity very challenging. They will not always understand the play on words because the vocabulary may be unfamiliar to them. If this happens make sure that these children are included in a supportive group when they are looking for jokes. It might help to tell them one or two jokes which they can then write in the book.

Assessment opportunities

Although this is not an activity which provides substantial assessment opportunities, teachers will be able to observe and record individuals' knowledge of different spellings and meanings.

Opportunities for IT

Children could use a word processor or desktop publishing package to create their own class joke book. They could experiment with different font styles and sizes to present each joke in an interesting way. They could also add pictures to each joke to illustrate it. These could be drawn using an art or graphics package, taken from CD-ROMs or other collections of clip art, or scanned from children's hand-drawn pictures and added to the written version of the joke.

A different approach would be to use a multimedia authoring package where children can combine text, pictures and their own voices in an electronic joke book. In writing such a book each page is linked to the previous and next page by an arrow or other picture (often called an icon). It is usually possible to get back to the title or contents page in order to go directly to a particular joke. This initial structure could be set up by you in advance so that children have only to make the links to each new page as they write the joke book.

To get started children will need to be shown how to use authoring software. Many children will have already seen similar types of presentations on CD-ROM and smaller versions on disk and will understand how to move around the book. If they have not seen these types of resources before, try to show them examples before starting. Children will usually need some support for their first attempts and it helps to plan the computer session when there is other help available. Initial planning of the page should take place away from the computer.

Each joke page can include text, which is entered, edited and formatted in the same way as most word processors. However, the text is usually placed into a frame which can be moved around the page to create the desired format. Pictures can be added from scanned photographs, children's drawings or other illustrations, directly from art or computer drawing packages, from commercial clip art collections or from CD-ROMs. For the joke book children could present the user with the joke and then an answer icon, which when pressed would reveal the answer, either next to the joke or on another page. For example:

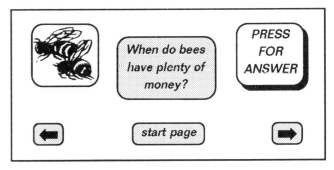

It is also possible for children to read the joke so that when the user clicks on the joke, they can hear it read to them. This is accomplished using a microphone linked to the computer which digitally records children as they speak. Other sound effects can be recorded and added in a similar way. If sounds are added, the files created can be very large, so unless you have a hard disk to store the book it may not fit on to a floppy disk. The final joke book can be printed out so that children can make a copy of it to keep.

Display ideas

The class joke book should be displayed where it can be used and enjoyed. It will be very popular, especially with those children who find reading long stretches of prose difficult. For these children, joke books make excellent reading material which will not only be enjoyable but will also provide reading practice and develop their facility with and knowledge of words.

Aspects of the English PoS covered

Writing – 2d.

Reference to photocopiable sheets

Photocopiable sheets 115 and 116 can be used to start the activity by providing examples of jokes that play on words.

Word families

The emphasis in this chapter is on the roots and derivations of words in the English language. Many puzzling things about English spelling have their origins in the history of the development of the language, so we have provided activities which attempt to show children why some things are as they are. Further information for the teacher is contained in the Appendix which offers a brief history of the English language.

The context of finding out about the roots of English provides a valuable opportunity for looking at other languages in the community. It is particularly important that children whose first language is not English are enabled to view their bilingualism as a positive asset and for all children to understand that other languages are just as valid as English. All children in Britain need to become fluent readers, writers and spellers of English and, equally, all children need to appreciate the diversity and fascination of all the languages that surround them.

A number of activities are provided for teaching about prefixes and suffixes. Though these represent only a small number of the affixes in English, the same activities could be used with different ones. Learning the meanings of prefixes and suffixes will enable children to understand some complex polysyllabic words. Similarly, the Kim's game activity based on vowel digraphs could be used with different vowel digraphs, or with consonant digraphs, consonant blends or indeed any letter pattern. The value of Kim's game is that it encourages careful looking at words so that the pattern is remembered.

NAME GAME

To enable children to identify constant letter strings in words.

†† *Whole class, then individuals.*

⊕ *Total of 40 minutes: 20 minutes in whole group; 20 minutes individual activity.*

Previous skills/knowledge needed

Children will need to be able to spell their own names correctly.

Key background information

This activity would provide a good introduction to the idea of constant letter strings. By Key Stage 2 many children will have become fully aware of letter strings; others will be moving towards this awareness and may still be at a phonetic stage of spelling (see Introduction, page 8). Once the activity has been demonstrated, it can be undertaken at each individual's own level, thus providing built-in differentiation, and the resulting word lists will reflect each child's current awareness.

Preparation

For the whole class activity, a large sheet of paper (A1 or A2) or a page on a flip chart should be prepared with two or three first names written across the top. These names should *not* be those of children in the class. For the individual activity, each child's first name should be written at the top of a piece of A4 card or paper.

Resources needed

Large sheet of paper or flip chart, individual sheets of paper for children, selection of different-coloured thick felt-tipped pens (for teacher's use), pens, pencils, felt-tipped pens or coloured pencils (for children's use).

What to do

Place the large prepared sheet of paper where all the children can see it, on a flip chart stand or easel. Ask the children to look at the first name and read it out. Then ask them if they can see any letter patterns in that name which they have seen in other words. When a pattern is suggested, ask all the children to think of a word which has that letter pattern in it. Write this word under the name with a different-coloured pen, then underline the letter pattern. Ask for another word with the same letter pattern, write this down in the same colour and underline in the same way. Continue until the suggestions seem to be running out. Move on to the second name and repeat the procedure, then do the same for the third name. When completed, the chart might look like this:

Claire	James	Amran
h<u>air</u>	<u>game</u>	<u>ran</u>
f<u>air</u>y	<u>same</u>	<u>gran</u>
d<u>air</u>y	c<u>ame</u>	br<u>an</u>ch
st<u>air</u>s	bl<u>ame</u>d	st<u>ran</u>ge
<u>air</u>port	n<u>ame</u>	<u>rang</u>

In each of the names here, other letter patterns might have been identified – for example, the 'cl' consonant blend in 'Claire', or 'am' in 'James' and 'Amran'. If children point out that there are other possibilities, let them suggest a second word list for that letter pattern.

Once the whole group seem to understand what is required, give out the paper or card with the children's names on and ask them to do the same with their own name. Tell

them to write the words below the name and to underline the letter pattern in a colour. If they work with two letter patterns they should use a different colour for each one. Some names, because of their length or unusual spelling, will be harder to work with than others and some children may only be able to work with two-letter patterns.

Suggestion(s) for extension
Children who complete this activity could be asked to do the same with their surname.

Suggestion(s) for support
Children who are unused to looking for letter patterns or are not good at spelling may have difficulty in finding words or spelling the words they think of. These children could work in pairs with children who are better at spelling, so that they are helped to complete the activity.

Assessment opportunities
The completed lists will show which children are able to identify appropriate letter patterns and this information can be used to plan further opportunities for the children to develop their awareness of common letter strings. You will also be able to identify which children showed awareness of rhyme. Some children may be aware that particular letter strings are sometimes pronounced differently: for example, 'Amy' might identify 'my' and 'am', both of which would be said differently from the parts of her name.

Opportunities for IT
Children could use a word processor or desktop publishing package to create versions of their word lists for display in the classroom. They could be shown how to select appropriate fonts and alter the size of the fonts to make a display that is readable from the other side of the classroom, but which still fits on to a sheet of A4 paper.

Aspects of the English PoS covered
Writing – 2d.
Reading – 2a.

NEGATIVE PREFIXES

To introduce the term 'prefix'. To focus on the meanings of the common prefixes 'mis-' and 'dis-'.

†† *Whole class, working in pairs.*

⊕ *30 minutes.*

Previous skills/knowledge needed
The children will need to have had some experience of looking at syllables in words, which may well have raised issues about the consistent appearance of common prefixes. The starting point for discussion of prefixes should be words familiar to the children, such as 'mistake' or 'disagree'.

Key background information
A prefix is a group of letters placed at the beginning of a word in order to change or extend its meaning. It sometimes happens that a word with a prefix has a very different meaning from the same word without the prefix (for example, 'compose' and 'decompose'), but most, including those used here, have a consistent meaning and in many cases the prefix will create a new word which has a roughly opposite meaning.

The meanings of these two prefixes should be explained to the children. The prefix 'mis-' means 'wrong' and 'dis-' means 'not' or 'away (from)'.

Preparation
Make copies of photocopiable sheet 117 on card, then cut out and laminate the cards in order to make them more durable. The two prefixes should be on different-coloured card from the basic words. You will need a complete set of cards for each pair of children. Make a copy of sheet 118 for each pair.

Resources needed
Photocopiable sheet 117 and thin card for the 'negative prefixes' cards (see 'Preparation'), pencils, copies of photocopiable sheet 118.

What to do
Give each pair of children a set of the 'negative prefixes' cards. The cards should be spread out on a table so that they can all be seen. Point out the prefixes 'mis-' and 'dis-' and explain that they are *prefixes* which can be added to the

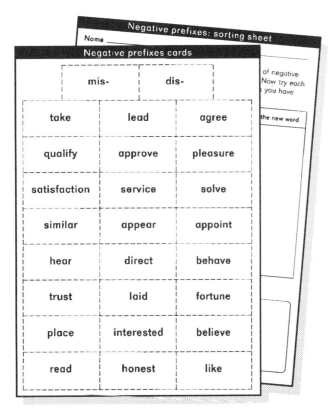

Negative prefixes: sorting sheet

Name _____

Negative prefixes cards

	mis-	dis-	
take	lead		agree
qualify	approve		pleasure
satisfaction	service		solve
similar	appear		appoint
hear	direct		behave
trust	laid		fortune
place	interested		believe
read	honest		like

Suggestion(s) for extension

Children who cope easily with this activity could be asked to make up some words of their own, using the prefixes 'mis' and 'dis'. These should be words which do not really exist, but ones which would be possible (for example, 'mis-' + 'compute' = 'to make a mistake on the computer', or 'dis-' + 'open'). Playing with words in this way is not only enjoyable but also reinforces the concept of prefixes being additions to words.

Suggestion(s) for support

Where children have difficulty in distinguishing which prefix would be appropriate for particular words, they should be given one prefix only, together with the set of words that can be used with that prefix, and asked simply to list the two sets of words.

Assessment opportunities

A record should be made for all children undertaking this activity, noting whether they have shown understanding of the concept of the 'prefix'. The sheets used for the sorting activity could be retained as a record of each child's understanding of the words.

Opportunities for IT

Children could be shown how to use the spelling checker which accompanies many computer word processors to check any new word they have thought of to see if it actually exists. An alternative to the computer spellchecker is to use

other words in the set of cards to make words which have a different meaning. The meanings of 'mis-' and 'dis-' should be explained (see 'Key background information'). Demonstrate the creation of a new word by putting together a prefix card and a word card – for example, 'mis-' + 'take'. Ask the children to write the two words on their sorting sheet under the headings 'Word' and 'Prefix + word' and then to write what the new word means in the third column. This example would look like this:

Word	Prefix + word	Meaning of the new word
take	mistake	something taken (done) wrongly

The children should then continue to try each prefix with each word, decide which one is appropriate (for example, 'mis-' + 'lead' or 'dis-' + 'lead'?) and then write down the words on their sorting sheet, as in the example. It should be noted that some of the root words can have both prefixes added to make two different words. These words are 'trust' and 'place'. (There are of course others not on the cards.)

This activity provides a useful context for learning the rule about adding prefixes to words beginning with 's': that is, the prefix is *added*, so there must be two 's's' (for example, 'dis' + 'satisfaction' = 'dissatisfaction').

When the children have finished sorting the words, each pair should compare their list with that of another pair and see whether they agree. Disagreements should be discussed and a decision made about which suggestion is correct. The lists should then be discussed with you.

one of the many types of hand-held electronic spelling checkers.

Aspects of the English PoS covered
Writing – 2d.
Speaking and listening – 3b.
Reading – 2a.

Reference to photocopiable sheets
Photocopiable sheet 117 is to be used to make a set of 'negative prefixes' cards for the children and photocopiable sheet 118 is for children to record on when working in pairs.

PREFIX PAIRS

To enable children to understand the meanings of common prefixes.

†† *Whole class, then pairs.*

🕐 *10 minutes whole group; 20–30 minutes in pairs.*

Previous skills/knowledge needed
Children will need to have an awareness of syllables within words and some experience of simple prefixes, such as 'un-' and 'dis-'.

Key background information
Many of the common prefixes in English have their roots in Latin or Greek words, and their meanings remain constant when they are attached to other words. Prefixes from Latin or Greek remain very close to their original spelling and do not get translated. An understanding of the meanings, therefore, will enable children to make informed guesses about the meanings of new words they encounter with these prefixes. It will also enable them to spell more accurately the words which have these prefixes. For example, a knowledge of the difference between 'anti-' and 'ante-' will help them spell words such as 'anticlockwise' and 'antechamber'.

Preparation
An enlarged copy of photocopiable sheets 119 and 120 should be made for display to the whole class. Further copies should then be made on card, in a size suitable for cutting up into individual word cards. Make up sets of cards with the prefix on one card and the meaning on another. Each set should contain no more than ten prefixes with their meanings. Use one colour card for prefixes and another for meanings. If possible, laminate the cards to increase their durability. A set will be needed for each pair of children participating.

Resources needed
Flip chart and felt-tipped pens (or chalkboard and chalk), photocopiable sheets 119 and 120, a set of prefix/meaning cards for each pair of children (see 'Preparation').

What to do
Using the display copies of the lists, introduce the prefixes to the children. Explain that many of them have been adopted from Latin and Greek and used with English words to change or extend the meaning. Choose one of the prefixes and ask the children if they can think of a word which has that prefix at the beginning of it. If a word is offered, write it on the flip chart or chalkboard, point out the prefix and underline it. Do the same with one or two more examples. If no words are

suggested, tell them one and ask what the word means. An example might be 'no-' – 'nobody', or 'co-' – 'co-operate'. You should point out that, when they are written, many words with prefixes are hyphenated and not simply joined together.

After the introduction give the sets of 'prefix pairs' cards to as many pairs of children as are to play. The cards should be spread out face down on a table. The first child should turn over one card of each colour. If the prefix and the meaning match, the child keeps both cards and has a second turn; if this pair match, they are retained, but the turn passes to the other player. If the cards do not match, both are turned over again and the other player takes a turn. The players should be told to try to remember where the prefixes and the meanings are on the table so that they can locate the ones they need in future turns. The meanings can be checked against the list of prefixes and meanings on display. The aim is to collect as many pairs of cards as possible. The player with the most pairs wins.

Suggestion(s) for extension

When the children are familiar with the meanings of the prefixes, they could try to play the matching game without using the checklist. If they succeed in doing this correctly, they could go on to make collections of words which contain the prefix(es). Different pairs could challenge each other to see how many words they can find for each prefix. This would involve using dictionaries, which would provide purposeful practice in looking at dictionary abbreviations (see also the next activity 'Greek and Latin Prefix Webs').

Suggestion(s) for support

This activity will probably not be suitable for all children in a class at any given time. Some might benefit from looking at a few of the most common prefixes (no more than four or five), learning the meanings and then locating one or two words for each one.

Assessment opportunities

Opportunities will be provided for observation of children's dictionary skills (see photocopiable assessment sheet on page 155). Note should also be made of which children understand the concept of prefix and which need more practice in this area.

Opportunities for IT

More able children could use an electronic dictionary, either the one with the word procesor or separate dictionary package, or a hand-held electronic dictionary to check any new words they may have made with their particular prefix. Many electronic dictionaries have other facilities which would allow children to search for all the words with a particular prefix. This might be used once the children have completed their list for the prefix they have chosen.

Aspects of the English PoS covered

Writing – 2d.

Reference to photocopiable sheets

Photocopiable sheets 119 and 120 have a dual purpose: they can be enlarged for display and they can be photocopied on to card to provide sets of cards for the activity.

Prefix pairs (1)

Prefix	Meaning
ante	before
anti	against
bi	two
cent	hundred
chromo	colour
circum	around
co	together/jointly
contra	against
counter	against
demi	half
fore	in front/beforehand
hemi	half
hydro	water
hyper	too much
hypo	too little
inter	between
intra	within

GREEK AND LATIN PREFIX WEBS

To familiarise children with the meaning and use of common prefixes.

†† *Large group, then pairs or small groups.*

⏰ *10 minutes whole group; 30 minutes pairs or small groups.*

Previous skills/knowledge needed

The children will need to be familiar with the idea of prefixes, perhaps through doing activities that involve adding prefixes to root words (see activities on pages 59 and 61).

Key background information

Many prefixes in English are derived from Latin and Greek words. Some, like 'super', which gives us 'supernatural', are

the result of Roman influences from the time of the invasion. Others are often the result of our having to find ways of expressing new ideas and technological terms, such as 'micro', which gives us words like 'microcomputer'. In this latter group, sometimes both parts of the word have Greek roots: for example, 'telephone' which comes from 'tele', meaning 'far', and 'phone', meaning 'sound'. In this activity, however, the emphasis is on the prefix, not the root of the word.

Preparation
Prepare a set of hexagon cards, using the template on photocopiable page 121. In the centre of each one, write one of the prefixes from the lists below. Using one of these, make a demonstration 'web', with a prefix in the centre and a word having this prefix on each of the six straight edges, thus showing six words with the chosen prefix.

Resources needed
Hexagon-shaped cards (see 'Preparation'), pencils, rulers, dictionaries for reference, rough paper.

Greek prefixes

tele – far	(mikros)/micro – small	auto – self
telephone	microscope	automatic
telegraph	microphone	autobiography
telescope	microcomputer	automobile
television	microbe	automation
telephoto	microcosm	autograph
telegram	microbiology	autopilot
telepathy	microelectronics	autocrat
telethon	microfilm	autocycle
telerecording	microwave	automaton
telecommunication	micrometer	
teleprinter	microsurgery	

mono(s) – one	photo(s) – light	anti – against
monologue	photograph	anticlockwise
monotone	photocopy	antibiotic
monotonous	photosynthesis	anticlimax
monolingual	photosensitive	antibody
monopoly	photoelectric	antihero
monorail	photocopier	anticoagulant
monosyllabic	photogenic	anticyclone
monogamy	photofit	antisocial

Latin prefixes

super – above/beyond	sub – under
superimpose	subway
supercharge	submarine
supervise	subconscious
superfluous	subcontinent
superhighway	subdivide
supermarket	substandard
superstar	subterranean
supernatural	submerge
superhuman	subtract
	subculture
	subsoil
	subscribe

omni(s) – all	ultra – beyond
omnibus	ultrasound
omnipresent	ultrasonic
omnidirectional	ultramarine
omnipotent	ultrastructure
omnivorous	ultraviolet
omniscient	ultra-high frequency (UHF)

What to do

Before the children begin work on the webs, explain to the whole group that they will be looking for words that have prefixes which come from Latin or Greek words. Tell them that many English words have come from other languages and that all the prefixes they use for this activity will be Latin or Greek words. Explain briefly why we have these words in English (see 'Key background information').

Now give each pair or group one of the hexagon cards and explain the meaning of each prefix. Ask the children, in discussion, to suggest any words they know which use one of the prefixes. If they have difficulty with this, give them some examples (see list on previous page).

Once the children seem to have understood the task and have some idea of the sorts of words they will be looking for, they should begin work on their own webs. Show them the completed prefix web (see 'Preparation') and explain that each pair/group will be making a prefix web. Make sure that each group has access to a dictionary and tell them to use the dictionary to look for words with the prefix in the centre of their hexagon. (Note: if you use the term 'hexagon' you could point out that it comes from the Greek word for 'six' because the shape has six sides and six angles, and that many mathematical terms have Greek roots.)

The children are likely to find some words they are not familiar with, so ask them, once they have filled up the web, to write down on rough paper what they think the words

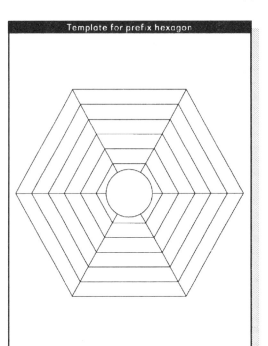

Template for prefix hexagon

mean; point out that the prefix will give them clues. Once they have done this the definitions should be checked, using the dictionary again, and the correct definitions written under each word in the appropriate space on the hexagon.

Suggestion(s) for extension

These children who readily grasp the idea of the meanings of the prefixes could be asked to find out about words where both parts have Greek or Latin roots (for example, words ending in '-phone', '-graph', '-photo', '-scope', '-cosm'). They could then produce a chart of these words, giving the meanings of both parts.

The children who have successfully achieved these tasks could be challenged to learn to spell the words on their prefix web, using the 'look–cover–write–check' routine (see Introduction, page 8).

Suggestion(s) for support

Children will be working in pairs or small groups for this activity, so they will be able to support each other. Those children who are likely to have difficulty with the more complex words should be given the prefixes which will be most familiar to them (for example, 'super-' or 'sub-').

Assessment opportunities

As the children are doing this task, observe their skill in using dictionaries and make a note of how they set about locating words and whether they are able to understand and use the 'headings, abbreviations and other conventions' (National

Word families

Curriculum). The 'Dictionary skills record sheet' (photocopiable page 155) could be used to create a cumulative record of each child's knowledge and ability to use dictionaries. Individual children's interest and enthusiasm for language study could also be noted and recorded.

Opportunities for IT
Children could use an electronic dictionary to check the meaning of any new words they have discovered.

Display ideas
The completed prefix hexagons could be displayed for future reference and as a focus for discussion about the origins of words.

Aspects of the English PoS covered
Writing – 2d.
Speaking and listening – 3b.
Reading – 2a.

Reference to photocopiable sheet
Photocopiable sheet 121 is a template for the prefix hexagon, which can be copied and cut out for use in the main activity.

SUFFIX RULES!

To familiarise children with the meaning, use and spelling of the suffixes '-ful', '-fully', '-ness', '-less'.
†† *Individuals.*
🕐 *30 minutes.*

Previous skills/knowledge needed
Children will need to have had some experience of using prefixes, which are generally easier to handle than suffixes. This activity should be used by children who, when writing, have misspelled words with these suffixes, or who have made some observation about the frequency of these word endings. It is intended for individuals who are at the stage of using these words, not for whole classes or groups.

Key background information
The suffix is a group of letters added to the end of a word to change the meaning of the word or the way in which it is used. The addition of a suffix may change the grammatical class of a word: for example, 'beauty' (noun) becomes 'beautiful' (adjective) when the suffix '-ful' is added. There are some fairly clear rules about how the spelling of the root word is affected when suffixes are added and the intention of these activity is to make these rules known to the children so that simple errors can be eliminated. The rules are given on photocopiable sheet 122. The set of rules is not exhaustive, but it provides a sound basis for learning about the spelling of words with these suffixes.

Preparation
Make copies of photocopiable sheet 122 on thin card and cut out the cards. Enlarge photocopiable sheet 124 and cut out the words to make a set of root word cards. Make a set of suffix cards (-ful, -fully, -ness, -less) on different-coloured card. Copy sheet 123 for each child doing the activity.

Resources needed
For each individual: a complete set of cards (see 'Preparation'), pencil or pen, photocopiable sheets 122, 123 and 124.

What to do
The player should place the five rule cards on the table where they are easily read. The suffix cards should be placed in a row on the table and the root words in a pile. The player picks one of the root words and the first of the four suffixes and checks to see whether they would make a real word if put together. If they do not (for example, 'happy' + '-ful') the suffix should be put back and the second one picked up. If these two do not make a word (for example, 'happy' + '-less') the next should be tried until a real word is found (for example, 'happy' + '-ness'). When a real word emerges, the rule cards should be consulted and the spelling of the new word checked. In this case rule 1 applies, so the correct spelling is

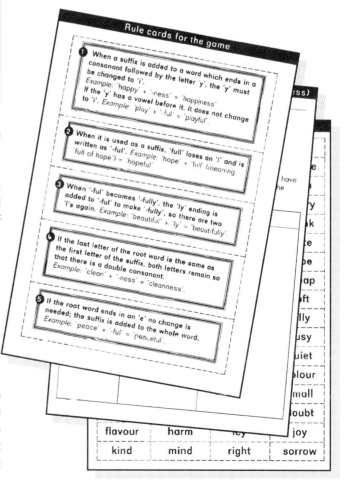

Rule cards for the game

1. When a suffix is added to a word which ends in a consonant followed by the letter 'y', the 'y' must be changed to 'i'.
Example: 'happy' + '-ness' = 'happiness'.
If the 'y' has a vowel before it, it does not change to 'i'. Example: 'play' + '-ful' = 'playful'.

2. When it is used as a suffix, 'full' loses an 'l' and is written as '-ful'. Example: 'hope' + 'full' (meaning 'full of hope') = 'hopeful'.

3. When '-ful' becomes '-fully', the 'ly' ending is added to '-ful' to make '-fully', so there are two 'l's again. Example: 'beautiful' + 'ly' = 'beautifully'.

4. If the last letter of the root word is the same as the first letter of the suffix, both letters remain so that there is a double consonant. Example: 'clean' + '-ness' = 'cleanness'.

5. If the root word ends in an 'e' no change is needed; the suffix is added to the whole word. Example: 'peace' + '-ful' = 'peaceful'.

| flavour | harm | | joy |
| kind | mind | right | sorrow |

65

'happiness'. The correctly spelled word should be written down on the player's record sheet. All suffixes should be checked against each root word, because in some cases a root word can be combined with two different suffixes to make two new words (for example, 'care' + '-ful' = 'careful', and 'care' + '-less' = 'careless'). When this happens, both words should be written down.

For a first attempt at this activity, the player should make about ten words. As he becomes more familiar with the rules, more words can be tried. It is not recommended that the full list of root words should be brought into the activity for any single game.

Suggestion(s) for extension

When children seem to have learned to apply these five rules, they could look at the suffix '-ly' and see whether the same rules apply. The same root words can be used. This should be offered as an investigative activity so that the player can test the rules with a different suffix; they should not be told beforehand whether the rules do all apply. (In this case they do.) Children may notice that '-ly' has been added to 'ful' to make 'fully' in words like 'useful'/'usefully'.

Suggestion(s) for support

This is a complex activity and it is not intended for children whose basic spelling is not sound. The application of the rules requires considerable support. If a child has used, but spelled incorrectly, a word such as 'beautiful' and you feel it would help that child to know the rule about words ending in a consonant + 'y', a small selection of relevant words should be made from the full list, and the child could carry out this activity, working only with rule 1.

Assessment opportunities

The completed activity sheets will provide a useful record of which children have both completed the activity and understood and applied the rules correctly. The completed sheets should be retained as part of the ongoing cumulative record of the child's growing skill as a speller.

Aspects of the English PoS covered

Writing – 2d.
Reading – 2a.

Reference to photocopiable sheets

Photocopiable sheets 122 and 124 can be copied and cut out to provide rule cards and root word cards for the activity. Sheet 123 is intended as a record sheet for use by the individual child.

KIM'S GAME

To encourage 'looking with intent'. To learn the vowel digraphs 'oe', 'ui', 'ue', 'ie'.

†† *Pairs or small groups of four or six.*

🕐 *30 minutes.*

Previous skills/knowledge needed

Children will need to be aware of some basic combinations of vowels, such as 'ee', 'ea', 'oo', before tackling these more unusual ones. They will also need to have had some experience of the 'look–cover–write–check' routine as a way of memorising words.

Key background information

This activity is intended to remind children that they need to focus on the *visual* aspect of words and that they cannot rely on the sounds alone to provide clues to the spelling. The same letter pattern often produces a different sound, so words having the same letter pattern need to be memorised in their written forms. It also provides a context

for practising the routine of 'looking with intent' (Margaret Peters, *Spelling: Caught or Taught? – A New Look*, Routledge, 1990) in order to memorise words. Versions of Kim's game can be used for any sets of letters, whether vowels or consonants, which the teacher feels the children need to learn.

Preparation

Using photocopiable sheet 125, sets of cards should be made bearing words which have the vowel digraphs 'oe', 'ui', 'ue', 'ie'. The cards should be laminated, if possible, in order to ensure durability.

Resources needed

A set of vowel digraph cards (see 'Preparation'), a cloth or large sheet of paper for covering the words, a timer (for example, a sand-glass or mechanical/ electronic timer), pencil and paper for each player.

What to do

If the activity is being carried out by a group, divide the group into two teams, each of which will use a different set of cards. No more than ten of each letter pattern should be selected for any one game; six is about the optimum number.

The chosen cards should be spread out in front of the team (or one of the pair) and they should look at them for the period of time allowed. (This could vary from three to five minutes, depending on the number of words used.) At the end of the specified time, cover the words with the cloth or paper. Each person then writes down as many of the words as she can remember, making every effort to spell them correctly. The lists are swapped with members of the other team (or the partner, if playing in pairs). The covered words are revealed again and the lists are checked against the cards. Points are awarded thus: for each person, two points for each word remembered and spelled *correctly*. Each team then adds up all the points for their members and makes a note of the total. The sets of cards are then exchanged and the procedure repeated with the new set of cards. The two scores are added together and the winning team is the one with the most points.

To play a further game, all words which were correctly spelled by all members of the teams should be removed and any words, from either set, which were incorrectly spelled by any member of the teams should be displayed all together, where all can see them. This time both teams look at this set of words for the allotted time and try to remember them. The words are then covered and all players try to write as many of these remaining words as possible. When they have finished, each person checks her own words against the cards displayed. This time one point only is awarded to each person having a correctly spelled word from either set. These points should be added to the team's score to decide on the final winning team.

Vowel digraph cards			
oe	**ui**	**ue**	**ie**
does	juice	fuel	pie
goes	fruit	duel	die
shoes	guilt	hue	field
toes	guitar	due	believe
echoes	guinea-pig	guess	chief
heroes	guide	sue	lie
volcanoes	guild	suet	niece
potatoes	nuisance	blue	piece
tomatoes	penguin	fatigue	shield
poem	ruin	vague	thief
poetry	genuine	league	priest
roe	quite	rogue	fierce
poet	squirrel	duet	cashier
hoe	suit	cruel	yield

SPELLING AND PHONICS KS2

Suggestion(s) for extension

Once children are used to this form of Kim's game and can remember words with these vowel digraphs, they could go on to make up their own versions of the game, using any letter strings, vowel or consonant digraphs. The act of researching the words will, in itself, help them both to notice and to remember the letter patterns, and by giving their sets of cards to other groups of children, they will be challenging others to learn the words.

Suggestion(s) for support

This activity has been planned as a team game so that children who have difficulty remembering the correct spellings will not feel unduly pressured. Those who do find this too much

of a challenge should be given sets of very common vowel digraphs and consonant digraphs to use for the game – for example, 'ai', 'oo', 'ee', 'ea', 'ou' or 'ch', 'sh', 'th'. Learning these will give them confidence to tackle the more unusual ones.

Assessment opportunities

A record should be made of those vowel digraphs, consonant digraphs and constant letter strings which each child is confident in using and can spell correctly. This information will be an important part of the cumulative record of each child's growing knowledge and skill in spelling.

Aspects of the English PoS covered

Writing – 2d.
Reading – 2a.

Reference to photocopiable sheet

Photocopiable sheet 125 can be enlarged and cut out to provide sets of cards for the game.

WORD DETECTIVES

To demonstrate something of the complex history of the English language and to stimulate interest in investigating word roots and origins.

†† *Whole class for introduction, then groups or individuals as appropriate.*

⏲ *1 hour for introduction, then occasional 30-minute slots.*

Previous skills/knowledge needed

Children will need to have some awareness of the variety of sources which have contributed to English, perhaps through working on an activity such as Greek and Latin prefix webs (page 62). Children without this knowledge can still take part because the activity is ongoing and they will gradually acquire it.

Key background information

The history of English is a fascinating subject for study and investigation. The language is constantly changing. Even now, new words are appearing, some created for new objects (such as 'CD-ROM') some absorbed from other languages (such as 'discothèque' from French). In the past language was affected by the invasion and settlement of people from other places, such as the Romans, the Vikings and the Normans. It also developed as a result of English people travelling to other countries and bringing back words from those cultures: examples are 'shampoo' from Hindi and 'umbrella' from Italian. The introduction of Christianity brought many words from Latin, and the invention of printing introduced many curious spellings of existing words. A brief summary of the main influences on English is included in the Appendix so that teachers can provide information or direct children to appropriate sources.

The activity begins with an investigation into the earliest roots of English, which is intended to act as a stimulus to further investigation on future occasions.

Preparation

A large map of the world should be displayed in the classroom, where labels or pins can be attached to it. Blank labels should be attached to the pins, or small blank labels should be made available which can be attached to the map with Blu-Tack. These will be needed as the activity progresses over several

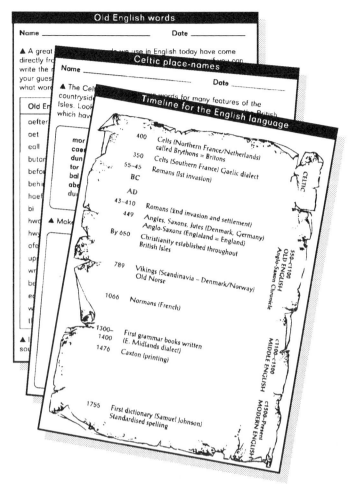

Old English words

Name _____ Date _____

▲ A great ... we use in English today have come directly fr...
write the ...
your gues...
what word...

Celtic place-names

Name _____ Date _____

▲ The Cel...
countrysid...
Isles. Look...
which hav...

Timeline for the English language

BC	400 Celts (Northern France/Netherlands) called Brythons = Britons
	350 Celts (Southern France) Gaelic dialect
	55–45 Romans (1st invasion)
AD	
	43–410 Romans (2nd invasion and settlement)
	449 Angles, Saxons, Jutes (Denmark, Germany)
	Anglo-Saxons (Englaland = England)
	By 650 Christianity established throughout British Isles
	789 Vikings (Scandinavia – Denmark/Norway) Old Norse
	1066 Normans (French)
	1300– First grammar books written
	1400 (E. Midlands dialect)
	1476 Caxton (printing)
	1755 First dictionary (Samuel Johnson) Standardised spelling

CELTIC

55 0–1100 OLD ENGLISH Anglo-Saxon Chronicle

C1100–C1500 MIDDLE ENGLISH

C1500–Present MODERN ENGLISH

into the farthest parts of Britain by the invading Romans and Anglo-Saxons. You could also explain that Gaelic (in Scotland) and Welsh are rooted in the original Celtic language.

Now return to the timeline and point out the period when the Angles, Saxons and Jutes settled here. Explain that their influence gave us the name 'England', the Anglo-Saxons called it 'Englaland' and the language 'Englisc'. The language used then, AD 350–600, was what we now call Old English and a very large number of the most common words in English have come directly from this language, which accounts for some of the odd spellings!

The children should then be given photocopiable sheet 128 which contains a list of common words written in Old English spelling. The modern spelling of these words should be written alongside. The children must guess what they think the word is; guesses should be checked by looking up the modern version in a good dictionary to see what is given for the derivation. If they have guessed correctly, the derivation should be shown as OE.

These two exercises complete the introduction to the 'Word detectives' activity. A list of some of the commoner words from other languages are given below. Whenever children encounter a word which seems to have a strange spelling, such as 'verandah', they could look it up in a dictionary to find its source and put a marker on the large map to show the country of origin. This part of the activity could continue as long as the children are interested.

weeks. For this introductory session a timeline, showing the main historical influences, should be made or photocopiable sheet 126 can be enlarged for use. Copies of the two worksheets (pages 127 and 128) should be made for each child.

Resources needed

Timeline (or photocopiable sheet 126), copies of sheets 127 and 128, for each child, pens or pencils, maps of British Isles, standard dictionaries which give derivations of words. (It would be a good idea to check the dictionaries in the classroom to see whether the information needed is given. If it is not, more detailed dictionaries should be borrowed.)

What to do

Introduce the timeline and explain something of the peoples identified. The information in the Appendix (page 91) could be used as a starting point. Begin by explaining that where the Celts lived we can find evidence of their language in the place-names. Give each child a copy of photocopiable page 127 on Celtic place-names and ask them to find examples on their maps of the British Isles. From the translations given, ask them to work out what the place was like. They will notice that the places are located in particular areas of the country (Wales, Northern England, Cornwall, Scotland), so you should explain that this is because the Celts were driven

SPELLING AND
PHONICS KS2

Origins of some words now used in English

French	Italian	Hindi
discothèque	vanilla	shampoo
café	opera	loot
restaurant	umbrella	dungarees
beef	studio	thug
boutique	pizza	bungalow
cinema	piano	verandah/
dessert	camouflage	veranda
casserole	solo	cheetah
Arabic	**Persian**	**African**
sugar	caravan	**languages**
assassin		chimpanzee
sofa		
mattress	**Persian/**	**Aboriginal**
sherbet	**Urdu**	**Australian**
alcohol	pyjamas	kangaroo
algebra		budgerigar
		boomerang
Spanish	**Turkish**	
tobacco	yoghurt	
potato		
barbecue		
canoe		
maize		

Suggestion(s) for extension

Almost any aspect of investigation into the roots of English could be followed up by children who are particularly interested. They could, for example, find out about Roman, Anglo-Saxon or Viking place-names and find these on maps of Britain, or they could investigate the influence of the Church and Christianity (Latin). They could take a theme such as food and look at different words for food items, to work out what this shows about the kinds of food which were eaten at different periods. A further strand worthy of development would be looking at the community languages of children in the class or finding out about and making displays of particular words in different languages. Even if there are not many languages represented in the class, this is a worthwhile activity, drawing on knowledge and information from parents, friends, teachers, older siblings or local people.

Suggestion(s) for support

Children who have difficulty with these activities should always be able to work with a partner who may be more confident in writing tasks. The investigation could be done by both partners, but the recording of the information on photocopiable sheets 127 and 128 could be undertaken by the more confident one.

Assessment opportunities

Most of these activities are intended to be open-ended investigations, but observations can certainly be made about children's knowledge of how to use dictionaries and their understanding of abbreviations (see Dictionary skills record sheet on page 320). Observations could be made about their interest and enthusiasm for finding out about English.

Opportunities for IT

Children could use a word processor to make labels for the class display about the history of the English language. They could be shown how to select appropriate fonts and sizes to fit on the labels. Children might also be shown how to add borders to their labels to make them more interesting; this is most easily accomplished using a desktop publishing or graphics package.

Display ideas

These activities provide opportunities for very effective displays about the history of the English language. Apart from the large map which can be added to frequently, other, more interactive displays, inviting children to investigate different aspects of English, would be very appropriate. The time chart could be illustrated and displayed and posters could be created using the information children have found out about word origins.

Aspects of the English PoS covered

Writing – 2d, 3.
Reading – 2a.
Speaking and listening – 3b.

Reference to photocopiable sheets

Photocopiable sheet 126 can be enlarged for use in the general class discussion. Sheets 127 and 128 are intended for use by individual children.

Curiosities

The English language is a fascinating subject to find out about and is full of curiosities. The topics covered here are designed to help children remember some of the spelling 'rules' and patterns of letters in words. Some of the activities explain the reasons for apparently illogical forms of spelling; if children remember the story attached to a particular spelling, they are more likely to remember the letter pattern.

In all the activities, we have tried to focus children's attention on 'the visual patterns of words' as suggested in the Programme of Study for Writing (2d), because this is perhaps the most important skill children need to acquire, in addition to knowledge of the alphabet, in learning how to spell. Activities such as word searches and lotto can be devised for almost any spelling pattern – for consonants, vowels, word endings, irregular phonic patterns or silent letters – and the concentrated 'looking' required will help children become familiar with the patterns.

Much recent work on the teaching of spelling (*Joining the ABC* by C. Cripps and R. Cox, LDA – Learning Development Aids – 1989) has highlighted the interrelationship of spelling and handwriting. Providing help with handwriting, especially joining letters so that letter patterns are learned 'in the hand' as well as 'in the eye', does appear to make a contribution to developing spelling.

Children must be offered strategies to help themselves to become better at spelling and must be motivated to pay attention to words. If the teacher communicates enthusiasm for words, then they will achieve this.

**SPELLING AND
PHONICS KS2**

DOUBLE CONSONANT WORDSEARCH

To focus attention on words which have a double consonant. To encourage 'looking with intent' at letter patterns in words.

†† *Individuals.*

🕐 *15 minutes approximately.*

Previous skills/knowledge needed

Children should have had some experience of doing this kind of wordsearch activity. Many activity books and magazines have wordsearches of this sort, and teachers will probably have used them as 'spare time' activities in the classroom. The activity of locating words in a grid will be familiar to most children.

Key background information

Activities which require children to look closely at words are helpful in developing their visual awareness. The more often they 'look with intent' at words the more the patterns of letters within words are internalised. Wordsearch activities are generally very popular with children and it is helpful to provide contexts which are enjoyable and which the children approach with enthusiasm. Such activities will not on their own be sufficient for children to learn about letter patterns, but when used in conjunction with other kinds of looking, they have a useful part to play.

Preparation

Make enough copies of photocopiable sheet 129 for all children who are to do the activity.

Resources needed

Photocopiable sheet 129, pencils, rough paper for making lists and squared paper (for extension activity).

What to do

Explain to the children that there are words hidden in the wordsearch diagram. All are listed down the side and all have double consonants in them. Use the term 'consonant' and point out the consonants in some of the words. The words may be hidden vertically, horizontally or diagonally. When they find a word, they should draw a line through all the squares in which the letters of that word occur. Some letters overlap; that is, a letter may be used in more than one word. Most children will be familiar with wordsearches, but for those who are not it would be a good idea to demonstrate what to do with one or two of the words. Once each child understands the game, he should complete his own sheet.

Suggestion(s) for extension

When all the words have been located, ask the child to choose one of the consonant pairs and to make a list of all the words he can think of which have that pair in them. Since there are several different double consonants, a separate list could be made for each pair. Once the child has made a list of one particular consonant pair, he could try to make up a wordsearch with these (on squared paper) and give it to another child to solve.

Suggestion(s) for support

For children who have difficulty in locating the words, clues could be given for each word, such as 'This one starts from the top' or 'This one goes diagonally, from left to right'. If a child still cannot see the words, he should work with a partner who is slightly more experienced in wordsearches.

Assessment opportunities

A note should be made of which children have a secure understanding and knowledge of the spelling of words with double consonants in them, and of which children show less confidence in this area.

Opportunities for IT

Children could use a word processor or graphics package to write and present their own wordsearch for other children to use. If they use a graphics package the children will need to be shown how to draw lines and add text. It is useful if the graphics package is set up with a background grid and the 'snap to grid' option set so that the lines automatically line up with the background grid. This option may need to be removed once children add the letters so that they can easily be positioned in the middle of the square of the grid.

If children use a word processor it may not be possible to add the gridlines. However, children should be shown how to position the letters using a series of tabs so that they line up correctly. If children try to use the space bar for this they will find that different letters take up different amounts of space (for instance, a 'W' takes up more space than an 'F') and it will be difficult to line up the letters down the page; even if the letters appear to be in line on the screen they will not be when printed.

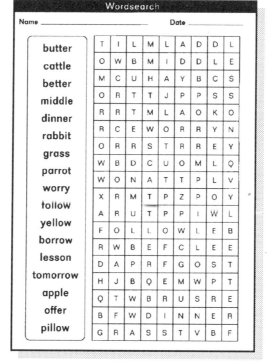

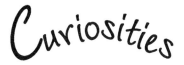

Aspects of the English PoS covered
Writing – 2d.
Reading – 2a.

Reference to photocopiable sheet
Photocopiable sheet 281 is a wordsearch for use by individual children and will provide practice in looking for words with double consonants.

PLURALS PUZZLE

To familiarise children with the plural endings of nouns ending in 'y' ('s' or 'ies').

†† *Large group, then individuals or pairs.*

⏰ *10 minutes whole group; 15–20 minutes individuals or pairs.*

Previous skills/knowledge needed
Children will need to have some awareness of regular plural endings 's' and 'es' before they are introduced to nouns ending in 'y'. This is simply so that they have a context for consideration of 'y' nouns. It is probably best if this activity is introduced and carried out as a result of errors noted in children's writing, rather than carried out with the whole class. In order to apply the rule, children must be able to distinguish between 'vowel' and 'consonant' and must understand the terms 'singular' and 'plural'.

Key background information
The spelling of nouns (and verbs) ending in 'y' often causes problems, but there is a consistent rule and, once children are familiar with the terms 'vowel' and 'consonant', the rule makes it easy to avoid errors. The rule for singular nouns ending in 'y' is: if the 'y' is preceded by a vowel, simply add 's' to make the plural; if the preceding letter is a consonant, the 'y' should be replaced by 'ies' to make the plural form.

Preparation
Use photocopiable sheet 130 to make sets of cards bearing the singular form of nouns ending in 'y'. Each set should contain about 12 words and there should be a mixture of words with a vowel before the 'y' and with a consonant before the 'y'. Make sets of ending cards, bearing either 's' or 'ies'. Each set should have the correct number of ending cards according to the words in the set. It is best if the nouns and the endings are on different-coloured card. The cards should be laminated if possible to ensure durability.

Resources needed
Flip chart or chalkboard, sets of word and ending cards (see 'Preparation'), personal spelling books (see the activity 'Making personal spelling books' on page 37), pencils or pens.

What to do
Make a list of those words which children have spelled wrongly when writing the plural forms or use an enlarged copy of photocopiable sheet 130. Place this on the flip chart and, with the children, go through the words, underlining the letter before the 'y' and pointing out whether each is a vowel or a consonant. Explain the spelling rule (see 'Key background information') and then go through the words again, changing to the plural form all those words with a vowel before the 'y'. Remind the children of the rule, then go through those words with a consonant before the 'y' and change those to the plural form.

Now give out the sets of cards to the pairs or individuals, as appropriate, and ask the children to sort them into those with vowels before the 'y' and those with consonants before the 'y'. Once this has been done, the children should use the ending cards to place the appropriate ending beside each word card.

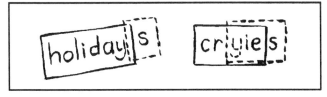

Once this is completed and the words have been checked by you, they should be written, as lists, into the children's personal spelling books. The rule about which words have 's' added in the plural and which have 'ies' should be written alongside these lists.

Suggestion(s) for extension
Children who have understood and shown they can apply this rule could be asked to make a list of *verbs* which end in 'y' in some tenses and which change their endings in the same way for different tenses. These would include:

buy (buys)	**try** (tries)	**cry** (cries)
carry (carries)	**marry** (marries)	**lay** (lays)
hurry (hurries)	**tidy** (tidies)	**fry** (fries)
say (says)	**play** (plays)	**stay** (stays)
annoy (annoys)	**copy** (copies)	**fly** (flies)
occupy (occupies)	**terrify** (terrifies)	**worry** (worries)

The children could make a wall chart of these verbs, for display in the classroom.

Suggestion(s) for support
Since there are plenty of nouns which end in 'y', children who have difficulty applying this rule can play the matching game several times with different sets of words. The words used should be confined to those the children have misspelled or those they will need to know for a particular topic. These should be noted in the children's personal spelling books.

Nouns ending in 'y' cards			
spy	key	lady	alley
baby	cry	tray	toy
story	storey	penny	ferry
jelly	abbey	puppy	lorry
library	journey	family	chimney
fly	strawberry	donkey	diary
dairy	quay	melody	monkey
party	holiday	enemy	birthday
monastery	turkey	quarry	allergy
jersey	display	fairy	berry
buoy	estuary	alloy	essay
territory	trolley	kidney	volley
railway	cowboy	valley	city
pony	body	hobby	cherry
discovery	mystery	factory	aunty

Assessment opportunities

A note should be made of whether individual children have understood and can apply this rule. Some children will need to revisit it at a later date.

Display ideas

The wall charts made as part of the extension activity could be displayed for reference.

Aspects of the English PoS covered

Writing – 2d.
Reading – 2a.

Reference to photocopiable sheet

Photocopiable sheet 130 can be enlarged for use on the flip chart and also copied and cut up to make word cards.

APOSTROPHE LOTTO

To reinforce children's knowledge of the shortened forms of words, using apostrophes.

†† *Groups of five or seven (one caller, four or six players).*

🕐 *20–30 minutes.*

Previous skills/knowledge needed

This activity should be used to clarify children's understanding of the apostrophe when it is used to mark contractions. It is better to introduce full explanation of its use when children have been observed using apostrophes, so some experience of trying to use contractions is the only previous knowledge needed.

Key background information

This game deals only with the use of the apostrophe to show contractions, *not* with its use to use to show possession (as in 'the man's car'). The possessive usage is best taught within the context of children's own writing. The most common error in children's use of the possessive apostrophe is the tendency to scatter them whenever they use plurals, and correct usage needs careful explanation, especially when the apostrophe is used with plural nouns, as in 'the players' cards'.

This activity concentrates on reinforcing just one role for the apostrophe. That is: when two words have been shortened and joined together, the apostrophe is used to show where a letter, or letters, has been missed out. Children need to know what the full form of these words is and to note exactly where the apostrophe is placed.

Preparation

A set of cards should be made by making enlarged copies of photocopiable sheets 131 and 132 and cutting out the words. The cards should be divided into subsets:

▲ those using 'not';
▲ those using 'is', 'has', 'am', 'will', 'shall';
▲ those using 'had', 'would', 'have', 'are'.

Each subset should be used for separate games.

For each game, boards will be needed on which are written the contractions of the words with the apostrophe in the correct place. The continual looking at the words, as the game is played, will help to fix the correct contracted form in the children's minds. A template for the boards is provided (photocopiable page 133). The words should be written in different places on each board so that the players will be covering different spots on the board. It is not necessary to include every possibility on each board. The boards should be laminated if possible. Rectangles of plain card should be cut to the same size as the spaces on the game board.

Resources needed

One set of cards (in a bag) for each group, one game board for each player, pieces of plain card for each player (see 'Preparation'); photocopiable page 134.

What to do

Before the game is played, explain the connection between the words on the boards and the words on the cards which will be called out (see 'Key background information'). Tell the players that the words on their boards are the *contractions* of the words that the caller will be calling out. They have to match the words on the cards with the contracted forms on their boards and if they see a match, they should cover that space with a piece of card.

The players should be seated around a table, with a game board in front of each one. The caller should be at one end of the table, with the bag of prepared cards. The caller reaches inside the bag and reads out the words on the card; she should then hold it up so that everyone can see it. If the full form of the words matches one of the contractions on a player's board she should cover that one with one of the plain card rectangles. When each player has had a chance

to check her board against the card displayed, the caller should put that card face down on the table, then take the next card from the bag and repeat the procedure. When a player has covered a line of contractions on the board she should call out 'line full'. The caller should then check that this player has covered only words which have been called out. If all are matched correctly, that player is the winner of that particular game. The game can be played as many times as the children wish, since each round serves to reinforce the players' knowledge of the contracted forms.

Suggestion(s) for extension

Some children will grasp the principle of the apostrophe's use in contractions very quickly and these children should be introduced to its other use, that of indicating possession. A simple first step would be to talk about the use of 'his', 'her' and 'its' to check whether an apostrophe should be used. For example:

▲ 'the man's car' – Could you say, 'the man, his car'? – yes;
▲ 'the girl's book' – Could you say, 'the girl, her book'? – yes;
▲ 'the book's pages' – Could you say, 'the book, its pages'? – yes.

If an expanded phrase, like these examples, makes sense, the apostrophe should be there.

Much more work will need to be done on the possessive use of the apostrophe, but this would make a good introduction. A worksheet on the possessive apostrophe is provided on photocopiable page 134.

Suggestion(s) for support

Many children will need the support of a partner in playing this game, so it might be introduced to a small group, who would play in pairs. There would still be one caller, but each pair would collaborate to decide whether there was a match with the words called and the contractions on the game board. Begin by using only the 'not' contractions.

Another possibility would be to use the game boards and the set of cards as an individual matching activity. The child should try to pick out the full forms of the contracted words on her board and place them on top of the contractions. When the board is complete, the words would be checked by you, and then you could explain any misunderstandings and errors on an individual basis.

Assessment opportunities

A record should be made of whether children are able to match the contractions with the full form of the words. The children's ability to use their knowledge from this activity in their own writing should be carefully monitored so that further reinforcement activities can be provided where necessary.

A record could be made in each child's spelling book of the definition of this use of the apostrophe, with some examples.

Aspects of the English PoS covered
Writing – 2c, d.
Reading – 2a.
Speaking and listening – 3b.

Reference to photocopiable sheets
Word cards for the game can be made from photocopiable sheets 131 and 132, which will also act as a checklist of words covered by the groups. Photocopiable sheet 133 is a template for the game boards and can be copied on to card. Sheet 134 is provided for the extension activity, which looks at the possessive use of the apostrophe.

KNIGHT'S KNOWLEDGE

To enable children to recognise and understand the function of the silent 'k'.
†† *Group of four.*
🕐 *Total of 45 minutes: 10 minutes introduction; 20 minutes playing the game; 15 minutes follow-up activities.*

Previous skills/knowledge needed
Children will need to have a bank of known words that they can spell. Through their reading and writing some may have commented on the unusual way that 'k' behaves at the beginning of some words.

Key background information
One way of helping children to understand why certain letters in the language are silent is to look at the history of the different letters and discuss the role these letters play when combined with other letters in certain words.

Silent 'k' has an interesting history, not least because in some cases it has not always been silent. In the seventh century – that is, in Saxon times when Old English was spoken – the 'k' was pronounced. The word for 'knife', for example, was 'kanif' and the hard 'k' at the beginning of the word was pronounced. Later on in its history, 'kanif' became shortened to 'knif'; at this stage, the 'k' was still pronounced. Eventually the word was written as 'knife' and the 'k' was no longer sounded. It had become silent.

A reliable rule with silent 'k' is to remind the children that when it is silent it always precedes an 'n' and usually functions as an initial letter, except when there is a prefix, as in 'unknown'. The number of words that start with silent 'k' is limited and most of these are listed on the 'Silent 'k' word bank' sheet on photocopiable page 135.

Preparation
Make four A3-size photocopies of the 'Knight's knowledge' game board on page 136 and mount them on to board. The children can colour in the illustrations before you laminate the boards. Photocopy the 'Letter 'k' resource bank' (page 137) and mount it on thin A4 card. Laminate the card and cut out the letters. Put eight letter 'k's into each draw-string bag or small box and label with a bold 'k'. Place a quantity of spare letters in a separate bag or box (these may be picked up during the game). Make four copies of each 'Knight's knowledge sheet' (pages 141 and 142). Make four copies of the 'Knight's knowledge cards' sheet (page 138), mount on thin card, laminate and cut out. One copy of 'Knight's knowledge: the rules' will be needed (pages 139 and 140), mounted on card for pupils to read or to be read to them. (The children could design and prepare some of the equipment for this game themselves as part of a Design and Technology activity.) Collect some everyday objects which have names that start with silent 'k' (see the word bank on photocopiable page 135 for ideas).

Resources needed
Photocopiable sheets 135 to 142 (see 'Preparation'), four A3 stiff word-card boards, glue, felt-tipped pens, laminating material, eight A4 sheets of thin card, four small draw-string bags or small boxes, four tokens (toy knights or coloured counters) and dice; collection of everyday objects starting with silent 'k'; writing paper, pens, pencils, drawing materials, dictionaries, word bank (for extension and support activities); cassette recorder with blank tape and headphones (for support activity).

What to do

First, ascertain the group's current awareness and knowledge of the silent 'k'. Are they aware of some of the words that have this letter? Which words can they think of? (See photocopiable page 135.) Use the collection of objects to illustrate some of the words. Where does the silent letter 'k' occur in the words? Can the children suggest why the 'k' is not sounded in words where it acts as an initial letter? Talk about the history of the silent 'k' (see 'Key background information') and tell the children that people in Britain have been writing the letter 'k' in much the same way for nearly two thousand years.

Next introduce the 'Knight's knowledge' game; explain the rules of play or give the group the copy of the rules to study (see photocopiable pages 139 and 140). Show the children the equipment for the game. Each child will have his own game board and his own token which represents a knight. He will also have a bag of silent 'k's. Explain that there is a bag (or box) of spare 'k's which can be picked up if needed as the game progresses. As they play the game, the children will pick up 'Knight's knowledge' cards which will tell them what they have to do. To start the game off, the players will roll the dice once each in turn. The person who throws the highest number begins and the others follow in descending numerical order. The children do not need to throw a six to start playing the game and should take only one throw per turn. Explain to the group that the aim of the game is to enable the children to practise adding silent 'k' to different words. This is achieved through the use of a story which starts the game off by asking them to help a small boy called the 'knave' to rescue his precious 'knife' which a dragon has captured. In order to do this, each 'knight' must overcome several silent 'k' obstacles to undo the 'knot' in the dragon's tail and return the 'knife' to its rightful owner. The story is provided below and it should be read out to the group before they begin playing. At the end of the game, the person who was the first to leave a silent 'k' on all eight 'Knight's knowledge' squares has won the game.

Suggestion(s) for extension

The photocopiable 'Knight's knowledge sheet 1' (page 141) is intended to test the children's growing ability to identify and spell silent 'k' words. The children could then go on to write their own version of the knight's adventures, using as many of the silent 'k' words as possible in their story.

Suggestion(s) for support

The game can be played in teams with children paired up. The 'Knowledge cards' have been illustrated to help the children follow the instructions. Ask other children in the group to help read the cards.

The 'Knight's knowledge sheet (2)' on photocopiable page 142 can be used, with photocopiable page 135, or the class word bank, to help the children. They could compose their own Knight's

Synopsis of the Knave's story

Once upon a time there was a knight who was very strong and very brave. The knight had been travelling for seven days and seven nights when he spotted a fabulous castle. As the knight approached the castle, he saw a small boy crying outside the castle door. The knight spoke kindly to the child and said: 'What is the matter?'

'Oh!' wept the young boy, 'I am the knave of this castle and I love playing tricks on people and making them laugh.' He sniffed sadly and continued, 'Yesterday, I played a trick on the castle dragon. I tied his tail into a knot. He was so angry with me that he snorted steam through his enormous nostrils and breathed great tongues of fire from his cavernous mouth. Then he saw my precious knife that my father the king had given me and grabbed it in his sharp claws. He's taken it into the castle and he won't give it back. Please help me, brave knight. If I don't get my precious knife back by nightfall my father the king will find out and he'll be very angry.' At this, the boy began to howl.

'Don't worry,' said the knight bravely. 'I'll get your knife back. Now what should I do first?'

'Go to the castle door,' said the knave and disappeared...'

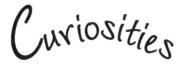

knowledge adventure, using as many of the silent 'k' words as possible and record the story.

Assessment opportunities

During the whole group introduction some children will demonstrate that they are aware of the silent 'k' and its special function with particular words. They may know that the silent 'k' normally comes at the beginning of a word and that it usually comes next to an 'n'. The children may be able to identify many of the most common silent 'k' words. In the game, the children will demonstrate their ability to read the words both on the board and on the 'Knight's knowledge cards'. When they use the worksheet they will reveal how well they are able to list the words and also spell them.

Display ideas

The games can be displayed for other children to play. A large frieze could be made which maps out the knight's journey to rescue the knife for the knave. All the 'k' words could be written on labels and stuck on the frieze. It could be given a title such as 'Knight's knowledge map'.

Many of the silent 'k' objects are everyday ones and could be collected and displayed for the children to look at. The written stories can be illustrated and compiled into a class book to be read at story time. Children can listen to the

recorded story independently on headphones and then retell their versions at story time.

Aspects of the English PoS covered

Speaking and listening – 1a; 3b.
Writing – 2d.

Reference to photocopiable sheets

The word bank on photocopiable page 135 contains a list of silent 'k' words, including some which are likely to be less familiar to the children, which can be used at the start of the activity, and this sheet can also be used for children undertaking the support activity. Photocopiable page 137 provides a bank of letter 'k's to be photocopied, mounted on card and cut out for use in the 'Knight's Knowledge' game. Photocopiable sheets 136 and 138 to 140 are also for use in the 'Knight's Knowledge' game. The 'Knight's Knowledge sheet (1)' on page 141 is for children to use in the extension activity; sheet 2 on page 142 is for the support activity.

THE FLOATING 'H'

To investigate inconsistent spelling patterns. To familiarise children with 'gh' and 'wh' spelling patterns.
†† *Small group.*
🕑 *30–40 minutes, depending on the players' level of interest.*

Previous skills/knowledge needed

Some familiarity with common consonant blends would be useful as a context in which to consider these more unusual letter combinations.

Key background information

One way to promote interest in the English language, and in the spelling system in particular, is to tell children something of the fascinating history of the language. If they know that there is a reason for some of the apparently illogical spellings, they are more likely to remember them. For instance, the modern 'wh' is derived from the Old English 'hw' in words such as 'hwaet' (what), the 'h' being pronounced, but the letters were reversed by French scribes tidying up the written form of the language to keep the same pattern as 'th' and 'ch'. Similarly, it is interesting to know that the 'gh' in words like 'night' was also the result of scribes trying to represent a sound which we no longer use, while the 'gh' in words like 'ghost' was introduced by Dutch-trained Caxton, using the Dutch spelling to represent the hard 'g' sound.

Preparation

Make sufficient copies of the worksheet (photocopiable page 297) for the number of children doing the activity. You will need one copy for each child.

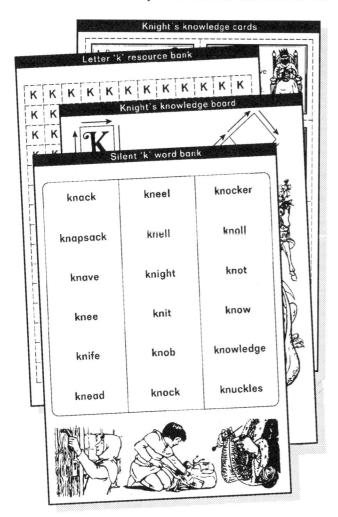

Knight's knowledge cards

Letter 'k' resource bank

| K | K | K | K | K | K | K | K | K | K | K |

Knight's knowledge board

Silent 'k' word bank

knack	kneel	knocker
knapsack	knell	knoll
knave	knight	knot
knee	knit	know
knife	knob	knowledge
knead	knock	knuckles

SPELLING AND PHONICS KS2

The monk's story

Do you know, when I was tidying up the classroom last night, a very strange thing happened. I was looking at the books in the book corner, trying to decide whether we needed to get some more poetry books, when I heard this voice coming from the table where you do the writing for your books. It sounded a bit like a Scottish person and it was saying, 'Och my! Hweer is the ink?' It made me jump and as I turned round I found I was looking at a very old man.

We don't get many old people visiting our classroom, so I was a bit surprised! I said, 'Hello, can I help you?' Then it was his turn to look surprised! He looked at me and said, 'Och, a woman! Hwat arre ye doin' herre?' Very politely, I told him that this was my classroom and I asked what he was doing here. He asked where the master scribe was, and he was obviously very confused.

I felt sorry for him so I took him to the staff-room and offered him a drink. He said he would like some ale, but as we didn't have any I gave him water. Once he had got used to me, he explained that he was a scribe and that he worked in a monastery in Northumbria. He explained that the same thing kept happening to him: he would be working away on one of the manuscripts and suddenly he would feel dizzy and, before he knew

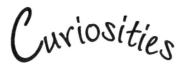

what was happening, he found himself in a different place. He thought he must have been dreaming, but he had seen some very strange things. He had been in a place where there were great big machines that seemed to write automatically; another time he had seen young people, including girls, who were wearing very curious garments and who seemed to be sitting in schoolrooms, but they were speaking in a strange tongue which certainly wasn't Latin!

As we went on talking, we both agreed that he must have been involved in some sort of time-travel and we decided that perhaps the best way of getting him back to his own time was for him to sit down and do some scribing. So I made him as comfortable as I could in the classroom, at the writing table. I gave him an old pen to use and the coloured inks from the art materials. We found a book of ghost stories – which he was very curious about because he had never seen a book which was printed rather than written by hand – and he started to copy out the book. I said farewell to him, closed the classroom door and, as it was just getting dark, I left.

This morning I found the story he had been copying out on the table where he was sitting when I last saw him – here it is! I've made lots of copies of it.

Resources needed
Photocopiable page 143, pencils or pens.

What to do
Begin by telling the children the story above. The monk's speech should be as near as you can manage to a Scottish accent!

The basic story can be embellished or changed according to the classroom context. (The teacher may not, for example, be a woman!) It does not have to be totally credible and the children are unlikely to believe it, but it provides an entertaining context for the activity they are going to do.

After the storytelling, give the children the photocopied sheets containing the ghost story (photocopiable page 143). Point out the words underlined and their strange spelling. Ask individual children (competent readers) to read out parts

of the story to the whole group and ask them whether they can guess the words, even though the spelling is strange. Explain about the old spelling of the 'wh' words and explain about the Dutch printers, following Caxton, who introduced the 'gh' into English spelling (see 'Key background information'). After this, the children should try to correct the spellings individually, by writing the modern spelling above the underlined word.

Suggestion(s) for extension
Many of the 'wh' and 'gh' words are used in this short story. Children who complete the corrections easily could be asked to make two lists of the words from the story – a 'wh' list and a 'gh' list – and could then go on to use a dictionary to help them locate others. They should be encouraged to find all the 'ough(t)' words.

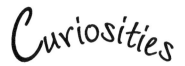
They could then work in pairs, challenging each other to learn the correct spellings of these words and testing each other. They should use the 'look–cover–write–check' strategy, described in the Introduction (page 8).

Suggestion(s) for support

This activity is not really suitable for children to do alone, if they have difficulty with spelling simpler words. If they are keen to take part, they should be paired with more confident spellers.

Assessment opportunities

After completing this activity, the children could be given lists of the 'wh' and 'gh' words to learn thoroughly and these could then be used as a spelling test.

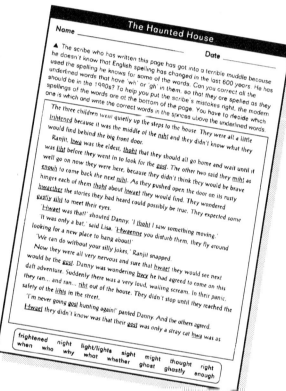

Display ideas

The children who have taken part in this activity could be invited to do drawings or paintings of 'the old scribe', showing what they imagine he might look like. These could be displayed, together with a copy of the story, accounts of how English spelling has changed and lists of the words used.

Aspects of the English PoS covered

Writing – 2d.
Speaking and listening – 3b.

Reference to photocopiable sheet

The story on photocopiable sheet 143 will help children to understand the origins of 'wh' and 'gh' spelling patterns in modern English. Each child taking part in the activity will need a copy.

HARD AND SOFT CONSONANTS

To raise children's awareness that consonants can be hard or soft and to enable them to talk about this.

✝✝ *Whole class, then individuals or pairs.*

🕐 *Total of 45 minutes: 15 minutes whole class; 20 minutes working individually or in pairs; 10 minutes whole class.*

Previous skills/knowledge needed

Children will have met and used the terms 'vowel' and 'consonant'. They may have noticed that some letters of the alphabet make different sounds in different words. When talking about letters such as 'c', the teacher may have commented on the sound of the letter being 'hard' or 'soft'.

Key background information

If children are to express their knowledge about the phonic patterning of words, they should be provided with appropriate terminology to do so. To help them analyse words effectively, it is inevitable that terms such as 'vowel' and 'consonant' should be used. As children become more experienced readers, widening their range of books and expanding their vocabularies, it is essential to support them so that they can deal with phonic irregularities. They will require terminology that enables them to make distinctions, for example between 'hard' and 'soft' consonants. This metalanguage will assist them as they reflect upon words that behave in unusual ways.

The focus in this activity will be on the letter 'c'. Many of the soft 'c' words come from the Latin 'cent', meaning 'one hundred'.

Preparation

Collect a set of objects (or photographs) which have names that start with a hard 'c': for example, 'car', 'cat', 'carpet', 'cartoon', 'camera'. Collect a second set of objects (or photographs) which have names that start with a soft 'c': for example, 'centurian', 'centipede', 'celery', 'certificate', 'circle'. Write the names of all the objects or photographs on the flip chart in a random list. On another page on the flip chart write the alphabet and also the words 'vowel' and 'consonant'. Photocopy the worksheet on page 144 for each individual or pair. Make copies of photocopiable page 145 for children doing the support activity.

Resources needed

A set of hard 'c' objects/photographs, a set of soft 'c' objects/photographs (see 'Preparation'), flip chart or chalkboard, photocopiable sheet 144, pens or pencils; dictionaries, blank playing-cards, rough paper (for extension activity); good quality A3 paper, photocopiable sheet 145, scissors (for support activity).

SPELLING AND PHONICS KS2

Hard and soft 'c' word bank

Hard 'c' and soft 'c'

Name _____ Date _____

▲ All these words have a 'c' at the beginning. Can you sort the words into the hard 'c' set and the soft 'c' set? The first words have been done for you.

cart	centigrade	camera
certificate	ceiling	circle
carpet	Centurion	computer
century	castle	caterpillar

The hard 'c' set	The soft 'c' set
corner	cell

▲ There is something interesting about the 'c' sound in the words 'concentrate' and 'concert'. Say the words aloud carefully and write down what you have found out.

What to do

With the whole group, briefly review their existing knowledge of vowels and consonants. Refer to the alphabet written on the flip chart and ask the group to identify the vowels. Draw attention to the two words 'vowel' and 'consonant' written on the flip chart. Hold a brief quiz to remind the class about vowels and consonants in words. For example, ask them how many consonants there are in the alphabet and how many vowels. Other questions – such as, 'Can you think of an object that starts with a consonant and ends with a vowel?' – will help them practise using the terminology. Once the children have had enough practice in using the two terms, conclude the quiz.

Moving on to the main part of the activity, explain that the focus of the session will be on the consonants, in particular on the letter 'c'. Tell the children that they are going to look at a set of objects (or photographs) of things that start with the letter 'c'. As they see each object it will be identified. They should listen carefully as this is done. Start with the hard 'c' objects and then move on to the soft 'c' objects. Ask the children what they notice. Can they hear any differences in the sound of the words, particularly at the beginning? Listen to their responses and comments.

Next take a hard 'c' object and a soft 'c' object and show the children the two words in their written form. Draw attention to the 'c' and ask them to say the 'c' sound at the beginning of each word to their neighbour. They may say that the soft 'c' sounds like an 's'. At this point, using these two objects, introduce the terms hard 'c' and soft 'c'. Hold

the rest of the items up in turn and ask the class to help sort them into two sets – the hard 'c' set and the soft 'c' set. Next turn to the random list on the flip chart, read the list through and ask the class to advise on how the words could be rewritten as two lists which would separate the hard 'c' words from the soft 'c' words.

Ask the children to look at the spelling patterns of the two sets of words. It is likely that they will notice that many of the hard and soft 'c's are working as initial consonants. Hard 'c' also occurs in the middle of words, for example in 'calculate', and soft 'c' occurs in words like 'necessary'. The children may notice the syllable 'cent' at the start of several of the words. Encourage them to guess what 'cent' signifies in terms of meaning. Explain that this indicates the Latin origin of several of the words on the soft 'c' list. They may also notice which vowel follows a hard or a soft 'c' most often (that is, 'c' followed by 'e' or 'i' is usually soft and 'c' followed by 'a', 'o' or 'u' is hard).

The children should now move on to the individual or paired work, using the photocopiable sheet on page 144. Allow 15 minutes and then stop the group and ask the children to share their findings in pairs.

Working again with the whole group, point out to the children that the letter 'g' can also be hard or soft.

To finish, play a brief quiz in which the children test out their new terminology by asking each other questions. For example, they might ask, 'Does "century" have a soft "c" or a hard "c"?'

Suggestion(s) for extension

Children who demonstrate a clear understanding of the main activity can compile some 'quiz cards' for the other children to use. Sample questions could include: 'Can you think of a word that starts with a hard "c" and ends with a vowel?' (Answer: 'camera'); or 'Which of these words is the odd one out – "cat", "centipede", "car", "carrot"? Why?'

SPELLING AND PHONICS KS2

(Answer: 'centipede', because it starts with a soft 'c'.) The solutions to the 'quiz cards' should be written on 'answer cards'. The children may need dictionaries to help them. The questions and answers should be written on blank playing-cards and rough paper should also be provided.

Suggestion(s) for support

(This support activity is designed for children working in pairs. Extra materials should be provided if more children are to be involved.) Those children who found the main activity challenging should work with the objects and sort them again into two sets according to the hard or soft sound of the initial letter. Once they have done this, explain that they will be making illustrated hard and soft 'c' word banks which will help the other children in the class find the words. Then read through the word bank on

photocopiable page 145 with the children and ask them to cut out the words and place each one next to the object it belongs to. Provide them with two sheets of good quality A3 paper. One sheet should be headed 'Words that start with a hard "c"' and the other 'Words that start with a soft "c"'. One child should select and draw a number of the hard 'c' objects on the hard 'c' chart and then stick the appropriate cut-out word next to the drawing. The child's partner should work on the soft 'c' list in the same way.

Assessment opportunities

The children will reveal their confidence in identifying and using the terms 'vowel' and 'consonant'. When sorting the objects, some children will rapidly identify the different sounds that 'c' can make and may identify other soft or silent 'c' sounds (for example, in the word 'scissors'). The worksheet will reveal the children's growing ability to distinguish the hard and soft 'c' in their written forms.

The extension activity and the quiz at the end of the main session provide an opportunity for children to demonstrate their understanding of hard and soft consonants. Some children will still be revealing weaknesses in their alphabetic knowledge and may find the terms 'vowel' and 'consonant' difficult to use. The support activity should offer evidence of their aural ability to distinguish hard and soft sounds.

Opportunities for IT

More able children could use a word processor or desktop publishing package to make further quiz cards for other children to use.

An alternative would be to set up an electronic quiz using a multimedia authoring package. The simplest approach would be to set up a page for each quiz card with the question in the middle of the page and an answer button next to it. Children can combine text, pictures and even their own voices on each quiz question. In making the quiz each question is linked to the previous and next question by an arrow or other picture (called an icon). This initial structure could be set up by the teacher in advance so that children have only to make the links to each new page as they create each new quiz card.

To get started children will need to be shown how to use authoring software. Many children will have already seen similar types of presentations on CD-ROM and smaller versions on disk and will understand how to move around the book. If they have not seen these types of resources before, try to show them examples before starting. Children will usually need some support for their first attempts and it helps to plan the computer session when there is other help available. Initial planning by each pair should take place away from the computer.

Each quiz page can include text, which is entered, edited and formatted in the same way as most word processors. The text is usually placed into a frame which can be moved around the page to create the desired format. Frames and text can also be coloured to create a more visually interesting display. Pictures can be added from scanned photographs, children's drawings or other illustrations, directly from art or computer drawing packages, from commercial clip art collections or from CD-ROMs. For each quiz question the children could present the user with the question, then an answer icon, which when pressed would reveal the answer and possibly a picture of the answer. For example:

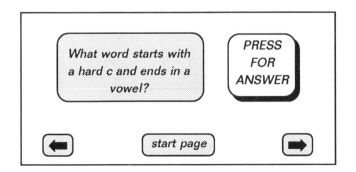

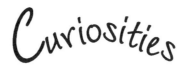

It is also possible for children to record themselves speaking each quiz question and combining the spoken version of the question with the textual version so that when the player clicks on the question, they can hear it read to them. This is done using a microphone linked to the computer which digitally records children as they speak. If sounds are added the files created can be very large, so unless you have a hard disk to store the book it may not fit on to a floppy disk. The final quiz can also be printed out, minus sound, so that children can have a copy of it to keep.

Display ideas
The quiz cards and answer cards from the extension activity can form an interactive display and will work best if used in pairs or fours. (Ground rules should be established for the answer cards.) The completed sheets compiled in the support activity should be displayed close to other word banks or dictionaries and the children encouraged to use them. An overall heading for the display could be 'The soft and hard "c" word bank'.

Aspects of the English PoS covered
Speaking and listening – 2a.
Reading – 2a.
Writing – 2d.

Reference to photocopiable sheets
Photocopiable sheet 144 will help children to discern the spelling patterns of hard and soft 'c' words. Photocopiable sheet 145 provides a basic word bank for children who need more practice on this activity.

SILENT 'B' CROSSWORD

To help children recognise and understand the function of silent 'b'.

†† *Whole class, then individuals or pairs.*

🕒 *Total of 45 minutes: 15 minutes whole class; 20 minutes working individually or in pairs; 10 minutes whole class.*

Previous skills/knowledge needed
Children will already have a range of words they can spell. In their reading and writing they will have met words which have silent letters, including silent 'b', and will have commented on them. They will have used the term 'consonant' in their discussions about words and their spellings. They may have some experience of the conventions of solving crosswords.

Key background information
Silent 'b' letters fall into two distinct groups: those that come before the end of a word, as in 'doubt' or 'debt', usually preceding a 't'; and those that come at the end of a word,

following an 'm' as in 'tomb' or 'comb'.

There is an interesting history to the first group of silent 'b' words which dates back to the sixteenth century. At this time, scholars wanted to show off their knowledge of Latin and decided to make a number of existing English words look more like their Latin counterparts. So, for example, they took the Middle English word 'dette' and tried to make it look more like the Latin 'debitum' by changing the spelling of the word to 'debt'. Similarly, the Middle English word 'doutte' became 'doubt' so that it would look more like the Latin 'dubitare'.

By sharing the history of the spelling of silent 'b' words with children it is possible to develop their interest in words and their origins. If children know the reason for the anomaly of the silent 'b' it is more likely that they will remember the spelling patterns of this particular set of words because of their 'curiosity' value.

According to David Crystal (*The Cambridge Encyclopedia of Language*, CUP, 1991), the exact origins of the first

crossword are unclear, but the form was popularised in the year 1913 by an American journalist called Arthur Wynne. By using the medium of a crossword, children will be directly focusing on the spelling of silent 'b' words through playing with language, thinking about the meaning of the words and manipulating the letters in order to reach the correct solutions. Crystal summarises the value of this kind of activity as follows: 'People delight in pulling words apart and reconstituting them in a novel guise, arranging them into clever patterns, finding hidden meanings inside them, and trying to use them according to specially invented rules.'

Preparation
Take copies of the crossword and clues on photocopiable page 146 for each individual or pair of children. Photocopy

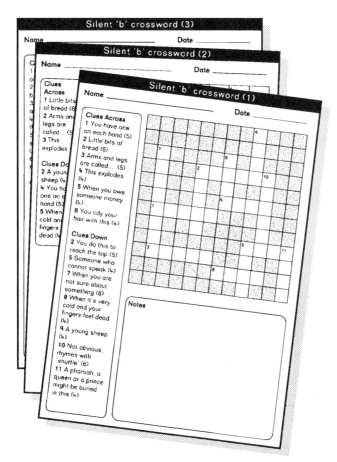

and enlarge one copy of the crossword sheet to use with the whole group; mount it on thin card. Then make a solution sheet by filling the answers in a copy of the crossword. Check that the class dictionaries contain the silent 'b' words being used. Photocopy the alternative crosswords on pages 147 and 148 (for support activity).

Resources needed
Photocopiable sheet 146, dictionaries, pencils, pens, flip chart or chalkboard, A3 card, glue; A4 paper (for extension activity); photocopiable sheets 147 and 148 (for support activity).

What to do
Start with the whole class together and explain that the focus for the session will be on a curious group of words that have a silent 'b' in them. Can the children think of any words with a silent 'b'? On the flip chart list the words identified by the children and sort them into two groups: those that have the 'b' preceding a 't', as in 'doubt', and those that have silent 'b' as a final letter, as in 'comb'. Ask the children what they have noticed about the way the words have been grouped. They should look carefully at the spelling of the words and the placing of the 'b' in each word. If they do not draw attention to the fact that the 'b' is before a 't' in the first group and that the 'b' follows an 'm' in the second group, then point this out to them. Add to the list any other silent 'b' words that have not been suggested (see the solution to the crossword on this page). Check that all the children know

the meanings of the words. (The word 'subtle' will need careful clarification.)

Next, briefly talk about the history of the silent 'b' (see 'Key background information'). Draw the children's attention to the words that have had Latin features added to them.

Explain to the children that they will be working for the next 20 minutes on a silent 'b' crossword. Using an enlarged copy of the main crossword and clues (on photocopiable page 146), explain the key rules about solving the puzzle. The children need to know that the crossword is solved by answering clues. Some of the clues go 'across' and some clues go 'down'. Draw attention to squares 2 and 5 which have clues for both 'across' and 'down'. The children need to remember that only words that fit the spaces can be written on the sheet; each square is for one letter of the word. Talk through with them about how to read the clues, explaining that the number in brackets indicates the number of letters in the word. Advise the children to write all the solutions in pencil first and to test any spellings they are unsure of, using the 'have a go' technique, in the space provided. They may use dictionaries to help them check spellings. Decide whether the children are to work individually or in pairs and distribute the photocopied crossword sheets. Some children will require a simplified version of the crossword (see 'Suggestion(s) for support').

When the children have completed the crossword bring the whole group together again to share their answers.

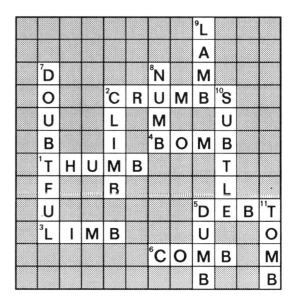

Suggestion(s) for extension
On completion of the crossword ask the children to work in pairs and to sort the words that they have written into two groups of silent 'b' words. This will follow the format that was demonstrated on the flip chart at the beginning of the main activity. They should write the words neatly for display purposes. Then ask them to see if they can compose two rules to remind others about the spelling of words with silent 'b'.

Suggestion(s) for support

Some children will find the full crossword too challenging. Two alternatives are included on photocopiable pages 147 and 148. Page 148 is the main crossword with some of the letters inserted, and page 147 is a reduced version using only words with 'b' as a final letter. The solution to the latter is given below.

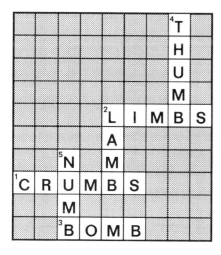

Assessment opportunities

The initial discussion will indicate whether children have noticed that some words have a silent 'b' in them. When looking at the lists of silent 'b' words, some children will comment on the distinctive spelling patterns. Working with the crossword, children may be able to spell and write the words directly into the puzzle. Others may succeed by using the 'have a go' technique and some will successfully utilise the dictionary. (Note how effectively they draw upon this range of strategies for solving the spellings.) Some children may write words incorrectly and be unaware of their errors. Note down children's approximations of the spellings and comment on any logical features, such as the use of phonic knowledge.

Display ideas

Cut out a selection of the completed crosswords and display them under a heading 'The silent "b" crossword'. Display the neatly presented word lists and rules compiled during the extension activity, with a heading which the children should compose. A suggestion might be: 'Can you remember the silent "b" rules?'

Aspects of the English PoS covered

Speaking and listening – 1a; 3b.
Reading – 2b.
Writing – 2b; 3c.

Reference to photocopiable sheets

Photocopiable sheets 146, 147 and 148 are for the crossword, the last two being simplified versions for the support activity.

DON'T BLAME MULCASTER

To enable children to recognise and understand the function of silent 'e'.

✝✝ *Small group or whole class.*

🕐 *This is a long activity and should therefore be spread over two sessions. First session: 20 minutes input and pair work. Second session: 15 minutes pair work; 10 minutes collating; 15 minutes writing.*

Previous skills/knowledge needed

Children will need to have a bank of known words that they can spell. Through their reading and writing they will have encountered the silent 'e' at the end of words and may have commented on it. They may have had some experience of working with silent 'e', which adults may have referred to as magic 'e' or silent 'e' in order to draw attention to its unusual role at the end of words. They will have had some experience of using the terms 'vowel' and 'consonant' and may have met the terms 'long vowel' and 'short vowel'.

Key background information

A familiar rule for silent 'e' goes as follows: 'When a word ends in a silent "e" the earlier vowel says its name instead of its sound.' This is true in part but unfortunately the rule fails to stand up when applied to short-vowel words such as 'give' or 'have', where the earlier vowel says its short sound and not its name. The rule, therefore, can be perplexing for children as there are so many exceptions.

A way of capturing children's interest in the irregularities of our spelling system is to look at the history of words and to consider explanations as to how their spelling came about. Silent 'e' has a fascinating history which can be pinpointed to one Richard Mulcaster (1530–1611) who lived through the reigns of several Tudor and Stuart monarchs, including Queen Elizabeth I. Mulcaster was educated at Eton, and was an enlightened scholar and teacher. He was the headmaster/high-master of two famous public schools – Merchant Taylors' and St Paul's. Among his pupils was Edmund Spenser, the poet, who later wrote *The Faerie Queene* (1596). Mulcaster wrote several books on education, including one of the earliest books on spelling. He suggested that if an 'e' were added to words of one syllable with a long vowel in them, children would be better able to distinguish these words when they came across them in their reading. Unfortunately, as time went by, people failed to adhere closely to his recommendation. The main culprits were printers who tended to use silent 'e' freely with words which did not fit Mulcaster's simple rule. The result was a large crop of exceptions, such as 'some', 'gone', 'done', 'give' and 'love'.

A way forward in working with silent 'e' is to help children categorise words into those which have 'short' vowels in the middle where the vowel usually says its short sound (as in 'give') and those that have a long vowel in the middle where the vowel says its name (as in 'home'). In this activity children will need to use the terms 'vowel' and 'consonant' and will benefit further if they can be encouraged to discuss vowels in terms of their being 'long' or 'short'. It will be helpful to have some discussion on this before the session. (The activity 'Long and short vowels' on page 22 will help prepare children for such discussions.)

In this activity the main focus will be first to help children recognise silent 'e' words in general and then to help them categorise these words according to whether they are short- or long-vowel words.

Preparation

Collect a set of objects (or photographs) which have names ending in silent 'e' and have a long vowel sound in the middle. These might include: 'plate', 'date', 'stone', 'bone', 'pine', 'file', 'mule'. Collect another set of objects (or photographs) with a short vowel: for example, 'dove', 'glove'. Select books on the Tudor period which contain portraits of Queen Elizabeth I and some Elizabethan gentlemen. Make a 'Vowels and consonants' sheet using A3 paper, mount it on to card and laminate it.

> ### Vowels and consonants
>
> The vowels are:
> **aeiou**
>
> The consonants are:
> **bcdfghjklmnpqrstvwxyz**

z Photocopy the 'Long-vowel silent "e"' worksheets (pages 149 and 150. Make an A3-size 'Silent "e" rule' sheet (see below), mount it on to card and laminate it. Use cold tea to dye sheets of A3 paper to give them an antique appearance for the presentation of the findings in the main and extension activities, (two sheets per pair of children). Prepare sheets of A4 paper and write 'start' words on them (see 'Suggestion(s) for support').

> ### The silent 'e' rule
>
> When a word ends in a silent 'e' the earlier vowel in the word says its name instead of its sound.
>
> | cap | cape |
> |-----|------|
> | tap | tape |

Resources needed

Flip chart or chalkboard, pens, sets of long-vowel and short-vowel silent 'e' objects (see 'Preparation'), photocopiable sheets 149 and 150, portraits of Queen Elizabeth I and

Elizabethan gentlemen, A3 paper, A3 card, glue, scissors, laminating material, cold tea for dyeing, dictionaries, rough paper; alphabet strips for support activity.

What to do

Spend five minutes introducing the **first session** and finding out about the group's existing knowledge of silent 'e'. Have they noticed that lots of short words have an 'e' on the end of them? Collect some examples from the group and list them on the flip chart. It is likely that the brainstormed list will include a mixture of long-vowel and short-vowel words. Separate them into two columns. Do any of the children's names end in silent 'e' (for example, 'Jane', 'Jade', 'Simone')? List those on the flip chart.

Show the children some everyday objects or photographs of things which have names that have long vowels in the middle and end in silent 'e'. Ask the children to identify the objects and/or photographs and add their names to the list of words that are already on the flip chart. Repeat the procedure with the collection of short-vowel words.

Next talk about the history of the silent 'e' (see 'Key background information'). Set the scene by showing the children a picture of Queen Elizabeth I and of how gentlemen dressed at that time. Emphasise the fact that Mulcaster thought up the idea of adding an 'e' to certain words in order to help children with their spelling. He added the 'e' to words that had long vowels in them. Provide one or two examples. Then explain how the printers often put an 'e' on short-vowel words as well. Again, provide a few examples.

Now explain to the group that in the main part of the session they will be investigating silent 'e' words. They will be thinking about the long-vowel words that Mulcaster created and the short-vowel words that resulted from the printers' influence. In order to do this they will need to use some technical terms. At this point remind the children of the terms 'vowel' and 'consonant'. Show them the 'Vowels and consonants' sheet (see 'Preparation'), and review their knowledge as necessary. Explain that in order to understand silent 'e' it is important to think about the difference between short and long vowels. (If children have not carried out the 'Long and short vowels' activity on page 22, the next part of the activity will help them.)

Return to the list of words on the flip chart and read them out with the children. First read the column of long-vowel

words and then the column of short-vowel words. Ask the children to listen carefully. Do they notice any differences between the vowel sounds in the two different sets of words? Select two words which have the same vowel in the middle, one long and one short (for example, 'name' and 'have'). First, ask the children to identify the vowels in the two words. Draw attention to the 'a' and ask them, in pairs, to say the words slowly to each other, listening carefully to the sound that the 'a' is making. Is it the same sound in both words? How would they describe the differences? The children may say that the 'a' in 'name' sounds like the letter 'a' in the

alphabet. Explain that the 'a' in 'name' is working as a long vowel. Contrast this with the 'a' in 'have' which is making a different sound rather than saying the letter name. This 'a' is a short vowel. Demonstrate to the children how to spot another long-vowel word on the list and explain how it was identified. Then ask the children, in pairs, to look at the list again and see if they can spot some more words that have a long vowel in the middle. As they report back, encourage the children to justify their analysis and to try to use the appropriate terminology. Repeat this activity with some short-vowel words. (When focusing on long-vowel words you can incorporate the use of photocopiable pages 149 and 150.)

In the **second session**, explain to the class that they are now going to travel back in time to the sixteenth century, to the world of Richard Mulcaster. They are going to imagine that they are helping Mulcaster make his collection of silent 'e' words. They will be working in pairs for 15 minutes, using rough paper and dictionaries to help them. The task at this stage is simply to list as many silent 'e' words as they can think of. As they make their list, they may find that some of the words are short-vowel silent 'e' words which the printers introduced.

Once the children have compiled their lists, ask them to compare their findings with another pair. First they should check that all their words are silent 'e' words. If any children have thought of words that start with clusters of consonants, such as 'stripe' or 'plate', share this information with the whole group as some children may only have been operating with initial consonants.

Next give the two pairs of children two of the prepared 'antique' sheets (see 'Preparation'). Starting with one of the sheets, each pair should try to sort their words into short-vowel silent 'e' words and long-vowel silent 'e' words. They should swap the sheets with the other pair to complete the task. The pairs should be encouraged to give advice to each other if they are uncertain about where a word should be listed. Finally, avoiding repetitions of words, they should write up a joint list neatly on two sheets of 'antique' paper. They should head one of the sheets 'Mulcaster's silent "e" words', and the other 'The printer's silent "e" words'. If there is time, the sheets can be shared with the whole class.

To conclude, use the 'Silent "e" rule' sheet (see 'Preparation'). Read it to the children and ask them whether they think the rule is a good one for the words they have compiled. They should agree that it works well for the long vowel words but that it is not helpful for the short-vowel words.

Suggestion(s) for extension

Before they write up their neat copy, some children will be able to take their two lists of long-vowel and short-vowel silent 'e' words and organise each list into different word families. To do this they need to look at the 'rimes' – the spelling patterns of the words that follow the initial consonant

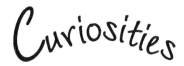

or consonants – and look for similar words. For example, children working with the long 'a' sound might categorise their words into the following families:

...abe	...ake	...are	...ate
...ace	...ale	('a' here does	...ave
...ade	...ame	not precisely	...aze
...afe	...ane	say its name)	
...age	...ape	...ase	

The 'u' family is the hardest to work with and this should be borne in mind when the children are sorting out their words.

Suggestion(s) for support

Working with one long-vowel sound (in this example 'a'), give the children a 'start' word, such as, 'game', and go around the group asking the children to suggest words that rhyme. As they give their ideas, write these on the flip chart. Do they notice which letters change and which stay the same? Select a fresh word, such as 'cave', and show the group that the 'ave' part of the word will stay the same but that the initial letter is going to change. Then, using the alphabet strip, systematically add different letters to 'ave' and ask the children whether the word made is a real word or a nonsense word. (The aim here is to demonstrate to them how to use the alphabet strip effectively in order to generate new words.)

Next give all the children different start words on different pieces of paper and ask them to use the alphabet strips to help them make new words that end in silent 'e'. If four

children are working in the group, they might focus on the following start words: 'came', 'cane', 'age', 'ale'. It is likely that children will suggest words that are homophones and with logical spellings that are in fact incorrect. These words should be discussed with them at the end of the activity, using a dictionary to help with explanations. The children are also likely to discover unfamiliar words, such as 'bale' and 'hale' (homophones). Again, use the dictionary to clarify meanings. The completed lists can then be written up neatly.

Assessment opportunities

The discussion at the start of the activity will reveal children's existing awareness of the silent 'e'. Some children will notice the differences between words with long and short vowels and may comment on this. Some children will use appropriate terminology to help them in their analysis.

By generating lists of silent 'e' words the children will demonstrate their awareness of how the 'rime' part of the word stays constant and the 'onset' – the initial consonant(s) – can change to make new words. They may work with a 'rime' systematically, by running through the complete alphabet sequence in order to create new words. If they remember to add silent 'e' to their list of words they will be demonstrating awareness of its role in spelling. Some children will be able to categorise words into word families. Others will find generating one family of words a challenge. Working with long-vowel words that end in silent 'e', children may make some links with the well-known rule quoted in 'Key background information' and used at the end of the main activity.

Opportunities for IT

Children could use a word processor to write the short-vowel and long-vowel silent 'e' word lists. They could add a brief account of Mulcaster's life for use in the class display.

Display ideas

By studying pictures of Elizabethan gentlemen, it should be possible to create a portrait of what Richard Mulcaster might have looked like. Surround the portrait with the 'antique' lists of long-vowel silent 'e' words and write a heading which reads 'Don't blame Richard Mulcaster'. The children could then write a short account of his life to explain the title. The short-vowel silent 'e' lists could be displayed around a photograph of an old printing press, with the heading 'Look what we did with silent "e"!'

Aspects of the English PoS covered

Writing – 2d, e; 3c.

Reference to photocopiable sheets

Photocopiable sheets 149 and 150 provide some of the possible word families for each long vowel with a silent 'e' at the end. There are of course many more for the children to discover.

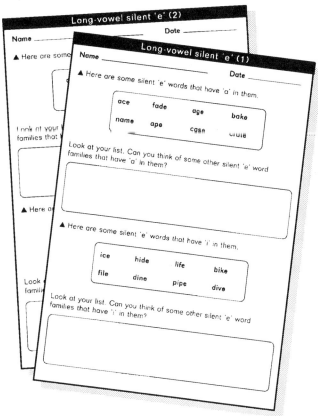

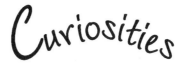

FASCINATING 'SC' CROSSWORD

To help children become familiar with more irregular phonic patterns.

†† *Whole class, then individuals or pairs.*

🕐 *Total of 45 minutes: 15 minutes whole class; 20 minutes working individually or in pairs; 10 minutes whole class.*

Previous skills/knowledge needed

Children will need to be confident readers and writers with an extensive bank of words that they can spell correctly. They will be working with a wide range of reading matter, regularly meeting unfamiliar words and widening their vocabulary. They will have discussed irregular phonic patterns, using terms such as 'vowel' and 'consonant'. In their discussions of consonants, the children will have heard the terminology 'hard' and 'soft' used – for example, in discussions about the letter 'c'. The children should have some experience of the conventions of solving crosswords.

Key background information

There is an interesting and unusual group of words that have the initial consonant blend 'sc' sound in them. These words fall into two groups: 'sci' words and 'sce' words. Many of the words will be unfamiliar to the children. They are often evocative words, such as 'iridescence', 'incandescence', 'fluorescent' which are all linked to light. The meanings of such words may not be immediately accessible and yet these are words that writers, artists and scientists use to describe phenomena in our world.

The words included in the crossword are intended to offer a challenge in terms of both spelling and meaning. The 'sc' sound itself is well worth investigating with the children. Not only are these words of value in terms of 'curiosity', knowledge of them will do much to enhance children's spelling power as well as enrich their vocabulary.

Preparation

Make enough copies of the crossword puzzle and clues on photocopiable page 151 for each individual or pair taking part. Make a word bank sheet on a piece of A3 paper for use in the support activity. The words comprising the solution to the 'sc' crossword can be used for this. Mount it on thin card and laminate it for use with the whole group in the main activity. Make a collection of objects (or photographs) which have names that contain 'sc'. These might include: 'scissors', 'scent', 'sceptre' (coronation picture), 'disciple' (picture from the Bible), strip light bulb or piece of 'fluorescent' card. Write the names of the objects on the flip chart or chalkboard, sorted into 'sci' and 'sce' words. Enlarge a copy of the blank crossword and clues (page 151), mount it on card and

laminate it. Make a crossword solution sheet (see below) on a sheet of A3 paper, also mounted on card and laminated. Photocopy the alternative crossword (page 152) for the support activity.

				¹S	C	I	E	N	T	I	S	T
				C								
	²F	A	S	C	I	N	A	T	I	N	G	
	L			S								
	U	³D	E	S	C	E	N	⁷D	A	N	T	S
	O			O				I				
	R			R		⁴P	I	S	C	E	⁸S	
	E			S				C			C	
	S		⁹U					I			Y	
⁵S	C	E	N	E	R	Y		P			T	
	E		C					L			H	
	N		O	¹⁰S				E			E	
	T		N	C								
		⁶S	C	E	P	T	R	E				
		C		N								
		I		T								
		O										
		U										
		S										

Resources needed

Flip chart or chalkboard, photocopiable sheets 151 and 152 (see 'Preparation'), A3 paper, thin A3 card, glue, scissors, rough paper, pens, pencils, dictionaries, collection of 'sc' objects or photographs (see 'Preparation'); good quality A4 paper, felt-tipped pens or colouring pencils for illustrations (for extension and support activities).

What to do

Explain to the whole group that the focus of the session will be on a group of words that is very unusual, in terms of both their spelling and their meaning. The important sound in the words is the 'sc' sound. (Write this on the flip chart.) Have any of the group come across this sound in words that they have read? Collect the children's answers.

Next introduce some of the objects and photographs. Ask the children to look at the objects as they are held up and, in pairs, to name them all. (Some, such as the photograph of the sceptre, may be unfamiliar.) Can the children spell any of the words – for example, 'scissors'? Ask them to 'have a go' on their rough paper. Write down some of their suggestions and then compare them with the correct spelling. Ask the children to use the 'look–cover–write–check' technique to memorise the correct spelling. Show them the written list of the objects on the flip chart. What do they notice about the spelling patterns? They should notice the 'sci' or 'sce' clusters of letters.

Now, using the word bank sheet (see 'Preparation'), show the children the list of words that they will be meeting in the session. Read through the list with them and ensure that they understand the meaning of all the words. Explain that they will be working for 20 minutes on the 'sc' crossword, which contains all the words in the word bank.

Place the enlarged blank crossword on the flip chart stand. Clarify with the children the conventions of solving a crossword. Explain that the words on a crossword go either across or down. Draw attention to the two sets of clues and link the numbers on the clues with the numbered squares on the crossword. The children should be careful not to put 'across' answers in the 'down' squares and vice versa. Point out that some squares share the same number for 'across' and 'down' (1 and 2). Remind them that the number in brackets next to each clue indicates the number of letters in the word. The children should use dictionaries to help them and rough paper to 'have a go' at spellings they are unsure of or to make notes of possible words. They should write their first attempts at the answers in pencil in case of making errors.

You will need to decide whether to work through the first few clues with the whole group to provide them with some examples. Depending on the group's confidence, distribute the crossword sheets either to individuals or for pairs to work on.

Once the children have completed the crossword, place the solution sheet on the flip chart stand and go through the answers carefully with the group. (Alternatively, the children could look at the solutions on individual sheets.)

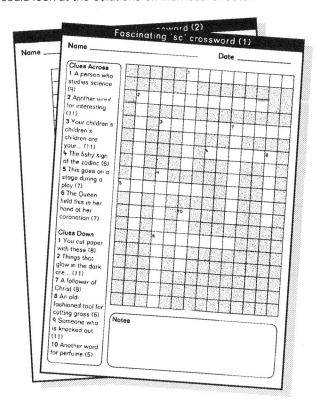

Suggestion(s) for extension

Organise the children into pairs and select two 'sc' words for each pair. The children should write the words neatly on A4 paper and carefully illustrate them. Include some words that were not used in the crossword. The children may also write definitions. The completed pieces of work will form the basis of an illustrated 'sc' word bank.

Suggestion(s) for support

Those children who find the crossword too challenging can use a copy of the word bank to refer to while doing the crossword or, alternatively, the crossword on page 152 which has the initial and final letters included. At the end, each child can choose one word that he particularly liked the sound of and draw the outline of the letters neatly and boldly on a piece of A4 paper. To make the word distinctive, the letters should be coloured in using felt-tipped pens.

Assessment opportunities

The children will show their awareness of the 'sc' sound through their suggestions of possible words. Once they see the objects and photographs, they may suggest other words that they have met in their reading. Through having a go at spellings it is possible to analyse the children's current understanding, for example whether they try to place the 'sc' sound in the words or whether they draw directly on what they think they can hear in the words. In discussions encourage the children to analyse the words using terminology such as 'vowel' and 'consonant' and see if they differentiate between the hard and soft role of the letter 'c'.

Their success in completing the crosswords and the range of the support materials they use will also indicate their growing range of strategies to support their spelling. Asking the children to learn some of the words by using the 'look–cover–write–check' technique will enable them to add to their stock of known spellings.

Display ideas

Cut out a selection of the completed crosswords and display them under the heading 'The fascinating "sc" crossword'. The work produced in the extension activity can be displayed under the heading 'The illustrated "sc" word bank', with the large colourful single words from the support activity stuck randomly round the edge of the display.

Aspects of the English PoS covered

Speaking and listening – 3b.
Reading – 2a, b.
Writing – 2b.

Reference to photocopiable sheets

Photocopiable sheet 151 has the crossword and clues on it for use in the main activity. The crossword on photocopiable sheet 152 is for the support activity.

APPENDIX: A BRIEF HISTORY OF THE ENGLISH LANGUAGE

This short account is intended only to highlight the main factors which have influenced the growth and development of English over the centuries. Numerous books have been written on the subject and linguists are still studying aspects of English. A list of recommended titles is included on page 93 for those who wish to pursue the subject or who would like to know more about particular events and influences.

The development of the language we speak now in the British Isles can be traced back through written evidence of the languages which formed the foundations of the English language. It is as we know it because of invasions and settlements of the British Isles over a span of about 1500 years, from 400 BC to AD 1066. This is not to say that there was no development after that, but the direct influence of other languages diminished after the Norman invasion.

The Celts

The Celts were one of many tribes living in Europe in the years before Christ. About 400 BC they began to leave central Europe, possibly because of harassment from other tribes. Some Celts from northern France and the Netherlands crossed the Channel and settled in England, Wales and Scotland. The dialect these people spoke was 'Brythonic' and they were known as 'Brythons', from which we get Britons. Other Celts from southern France settled in Ireland and kept their own dialect, now called Gaelic.

The Celtic influence can still be seen in place-names throughout the British Isles, where we can find Celtic words for features of the landscape (see the activity 'Word detectives' on page 68). Many of the place-names which have Celtic words in them are located in particular areas (Wales, Cornwall, Cumbria and south-west Scotland). This is because later invasions of Romans, Angles, Saxons and Jutes – who arrived in the south and east of Britain – caused the Celts to move as far away as possible and finally settle around the edges of Britain!

The Celts had their own writing system which has survived as inscriptions on stone, mainly in Wales and Ireland. Later, Celtic monks adopted the Roman alphabet, and its use became widespread because it was easier to write than the Celtic script; this is the basis of our present alphabet.

The Romans

For 300 years after they settled in Britain, the Celts were undisturbed, until the Romans began to attack the islands in the first century BC. In AD 43 Britannia (as the Romans named it) was conquered and became part of the Roman Empire. The Romans ruled Britain until AD 410, but remained remarkably separate from the Britons. They built roads and travelled throughout the country (though not into Scotland).

We can tell where they went from remains of their building, and from a few place-names which were adopted and slightly changed by later invaders. For instance, the Latin word 'castra' (a military camp) was adopted by the Celts, and later by the Anglo-Saxons, to survive in such place-names as Lancaster, Chester, Manchester and Chichester. But there was little real Latin influence on the Celtic language at this time.

Angles, Saxons and Jutes

After the Romans left there were further invasions, starting in AD 449, by tribes who spoke a Germanic dialect of the Celtic language – Angles, Saxons and Jutes. They settled and gradually wiped out from most of the country all trace of the Celtic Britons, who fled to the most distant ports of the British Isles. These people became known as the Anglo-Saxons and they gave the name of Englaland to their new home; they and their language were Englisc. From this, we get England and English. They called the Britons 'wealas' (which meant foreigners!) and it is from this that we have the name Wales. Over a period of nearly 350 years the Anglo-Saxons made England their own and created seven kingdoms which have names that still survive: Wessex (West Saxons), Essex (East Saxons), Sussex (South Saxons), East Anglia (mainly Angles), Mercia (mainly Angles), Kent (mainly Jutes) and Northumbria, the land north of the Humber (mainly Angles).

All the surviving Roman and Celtic place-names were changed by the Anglo-Saxons to their own language. This language we now know as Old English (in dictionary derivations it is abbreviated to OE). Some Old English words are commonly found in place-names today, such as: 'ham' – homestead or village; 'ing' – follower of; 'ton/tun' – enclosure or village; 'wic' – dairy farm or camp; 'burh/burg and ceaster' – fortress, walled town or fortified place. We can see these words in places like Birmingham (the home of the follower of Beorma), Chiswick (the dairy farm for cheese), Norton (the north village), Newbury (the new fortress) and many others. An extension of the activity 'Word detectives' on page 68 which includes looking for Celtic place-names could be to look for Old English names; there are several useful reference books on place-names, their meanings and derivation.

Old English

We know a good deal about Old English vocabulary and word forms because writing from that time has survived. Some was written in runes, like the famous poem 'The Dream of the Rood', which was carved in runes on a stone cross. In fact the Old English verb 'writan', from which we get 'write', means 'to scratch runes into bark'. Other writing, chiefly that done by monks, used the Roman alphabet.

Perhaps the most significant document in Old English is the Anglo-Saxon Chronicle, which is a historical record of the events in Britain from the arrival of the Angles, Saxons and Jutes, in 449, through six centuries. It is known that

King Alfred was the originator of the Chronicle and some believe that he may have written the events of his own reign himself! The events were written down over a period of some 300 years and because of this the Chronicle is a useful record of the changes which took place in the language over that time. If the Chronicle is the best of Anglo-Saxon prose, the epic of *Beowulf*, which was written down around 700, must be the finest poetry from this time. It is thanks to the Anglo-Saxon Chronicle that we know so much about the later invaders of the British Isles; it records, for instance, the first Viking raids in 789.

The Vikings

The Vikings were from Scandinavia (Danes and Norwegians). Their raids on the British Isles went on for more than 200 years but eventually they settled to live alongside the English. Their language, Old Norse, had the same Germanic roots as English, so the two languages merged quite successfully. If we look at place-names again, the influence of Old Norse can be clearly seen in the elements of many names:

▲ 'thorpe' – farm or small village (for example, Scunthorpe);

▲ 'stoke' – holy place or monastery (for example, Stoke-on-Trent);

▲ 'toft' – the site of a house and outbuildings (for example, Lowestoft);

▲ 'by' – village or homestead (for example, Derby, Rugby, Whitby);

▲ 'thwaite' – meadow or fenced-off land (for example, Bassenthwaite, Braithwaite).

There are many Norse place-names in the north-east of England because this area (north of the Midlands and including East Anglia) became the 'Danelaw': a separate kingdom from the areas to the south and west, and ruled by the Danes. Some Norse words have survived alongside Old English words: for example, 'skirt' (Norse), along with 'shirt' (Old English), 'anger' (Norse), along with 'wrath' (Old English). Others, such as 'leg', 'flat', 'let', 'give', 'take', 'die', 'egg' and 'sky', remained and became part of the English language. Most of the Old Norse words, however, died out.

Christianity

At the same time that the Anglo-Saxons, and later the Vikings, were establishing themselves, Christianity was spreading throughout the British Isles. Early on, the use of Latin in monasteries for producing manuscripts led to the wider introduction of the Roman alphabet. By AD 650 Christianity was established throughout the country and with it there came a whole host of new words. The Latin language provided the basis for thousands of words and parts of words which were added to the existing English language. Monks began to translate the Bible into English, and where there was no appropriate Old English word, Latin words were used instead. Vocabulary to do with religion and worship – such as 'altar', 'candle', 'mass', 'monk', 'priest', 'psalm', 'temple',

'minister', 'disciple', 'abbot', 'bishop', 'wine', 'angel' – arrived in great profusion. The Church also had a strong influence on everyday life and many words for clothing, food and household items were borrowed from Latin: a few examples are 'cap', 'silk', 'chest', 'mat', 'pear', 'radish', 'cook', 'lily' and 'plant'.

The Normans (French)

The last invasion of the British Isles, in 1066, brought the influence of French. The Normans defeated the English king Harold and ruled England for the next 200 years. The people in power in the country spoke only French and a huge gap grew between the upper classes, who used French, and the ordinary people, who spoke only English. At this time, words associated with ruling the country entered the language – such words as 'court', 'castle', 'cardinal', 'prison', 'tax', 'justice', 'arrest', 'army' and 'navy'. Once again, some words from Old English survived alongside the French to give us alternatives: for example, 'yearly' (OE), 'annual' (F); 'might' (OE), 'power' (F); 'smell' (OE), 'odour' (F); 'ask' (OE), 'question' (F). In the 200 years of French rule there was very little writing in English; Latin was used as a common language when the English and their French rulers could not understand each other. Between 1066 and 1500 thousands of new words entered the language from French, and English began to look much more like modern English. This was the time of Middle English, the language in which the poet Chaucer wrote *The Canterbury Tales* (1387).

The beginning of standard English

As the power of the Normans declined in the thirteenth century, English began to be used again in government and in literature. At this time there were six main regional varieties of Middle English and the language in different parts of the country used different vocabulary, grammar and pronunciation. As English was used more and more for official documents, a move towards a common written form of the language became evident. One dialect, that of the East Midlands – an area bounded by a triangle formed by the two major universities, Oxford and Cambridge, and London, the seat of power – acquired a higher status than the others. Thus, when the first 'grammar books' were written between 1300 and 1400, the grammar of this high-status dialect came to be seen as more correct.

Spelling

Spelling, too, began to be more standardised with the advent of printing in 1476. Caxton's influence on spelling was sometimes informed by his knowledge of Dutch (see the activity 'The floating "h"' on page 78) from which he introduced some curious forms of spelling. For example, he thought it necessary to use 'gh' to represent the hard 'g' sound of words like 'ghost'. Other printers, seeking a symbol to represent the 'f' sound of words like 'cough' and 'laugh',

came up with 'gh', which has persisted to this day. It was not until the first widely used dictionary (that of Samuel Johnson) was published in 1755, that printers had a way of checking whether a spelling was 'correct'. For a very long time handwritten documents continued to have non-standard spellings, even of people's names, but Johnson's dictionary established most of the forms of spelling we use today. It is interesting to reflect that these 'correct' versions were one man's choices!

Trade and exploration

Since the fifteenth century a further influence on the English language has been trade. For hundreds of years England was one of the world's great exploring and trading nations. Not only did new products, plants and artefacts arrive in Britain complete with their names (like 'tobacco', 'potato', 'cocoa'), but the explorers and traders learned new words in the countries they visited and as these words were brought back they were added to the English language. Many Italian words appeared in the sixteenth century as a result of travel. These were words like 'opera', 'piano', 'inferno', 'volcano', 'carnival', 'umbrella' and 'stiletto'.

The growth of the British Empire in the nineteenth century brought new words from countries such as India (whose languages include Hindi, Bengali, Gujarati and Punjabi): 'chutney', 'bangle', 'shampoo', 'dinghy' and 'gymkhana' all come from this source. In addition, people who have come to live and work in Britain, like the Dutch weavers and artists who settled in the fenlands, have added words to our vocabulary: 'scone', 'deck', 'hoist', 'boom', 'landscape', 'spool' and 'groove' are examples.

Modern influences

The English language is still absorbing elements of other languages as well as other dialects and forms of English that have developed throughout the world. English-speaking people are to be found in every continent and their use of the language is often very different from standard British English. Some of the forms of English used by Americans, Australians, Canadians, South Africans and so on have come back to England and have been absorbed into our speech. The dialects of the Caribbean, which were brought to England by the first immigrants, have themselves changed and developed to become British Black English, and this, in turn, has been adopted by young people from other ethnic groups.

English has always been a 'sponge-like' language able to soak up elements of all the languages that English people have encountered. It has never been, and never will be, static and set in stone. Many words, and even some grammatical forms, which were used only 40 years ago have changed; young people do not often refer to 'the wireless', 'gramophones' or 'frocks' in the 1990s, though of course some older people still do. Children will be able to talk about the current 'in' words and the vocabulary of *their* time:

discussion of these words and where they come from can be an effective introduction to finding out about the English language over the centuries.

Useful books about the history of English

Baugh, A.C. and Cable, T. (1990) *A History of the English Language*, Routledge.
Crystal, D. (1991) *The Cambridge Encyclopaedia of Language*, Cambridge University Press.
Fuller, S. *et al.* (1990) *Language File*, Longman.
Matthews, C.M. (1979) *How Place Names Began*, Beaver Books (Hamlyn).
McCrum, R. *et al.* (1992, revised edition) *The Story of English*, Faber.
Richmond, J. *et al.* (1982) *The Languages Book*, English and Media Centre.

GLOSSARY OF ESSENTIAL TERMS

Alliteration	a sequence of words beginning with the same sound.
Apostrophe	(a) denotes possession, as in 'John's money'; (b) indicates a contraction or shortening of words, as in 'Don't touch'.
Compound word	two or more words that combine to form a new word.
Consonant	all the letters of the alphabet except the vowels. Consonants can be hard or soft. Some consonants can be both hard and soft, for example 'c' as in 'cat' (hard) and 'ceiling' (soft).
Consonant digraph	two consonants that combine to make a new sound, such as 'ch', 'sh', 'wh', 'th', 'ph', 'gh', 'ng'.
Diphthong	two vowel *sounds* that combine together to make a single new sound within a syllable, for example 'oil', 'toy', 'they', 'out', 'cow', 'few' ('w' functions as a vowel).
Doubled consonant	two identical consonants making the sound of one consonant, for example 'bb', 'dd', 'ff'.
Final consonant	a consonant that ends a word, for example 'ma__t__'.

GLOSSARY OF ESSENTIAL TERMS (CONT.)

Grapheme — the smallest unit of sound represented as a written symbol. The 26 letters of the alphabet are graphemes. By changing a grapheme in a word it is possible to change the meaning, as in '[c]at' to '[b]at'.

Graphic knowledge — 'what can be learned about word meanings and parts of words from consistent letter patterns' (*English in the National Curriculum*, DFE, 1995).

Homophone — words that have the same pronunciation but different meanings and spellings.

Initial consonant — a consonant that begins a word, for example '<u>b</u>oy'.

Initial consonant blend — the consonants retain their original sounds but run, or are 'blended', together, for example 'bl', 'br', 'cl', 'dr', 'pl', 'fr'.

Long vowel sound — when the vowel sounds like its name, for example as in 'l<u>a</u>te'.

Metalanguage — a language with which to talk about language. Children need to meet essential terminology in order to help them talk about words.

Monosyllabic — a word of one syllable, for example 'dog'.

Onset and rime — 'onset' is the consonant or cluster of consonants at the beginning of a word or syllable, and 'rime' is the rest of the word or syllable, which enables the word to rhyme with other words.

Phoneme — the smallest unit of sound that can be spoken or heard, such as 'c' as in 'cat'. Over 40 vowel and consonant sounds have been identified in English.

Phonic knowledge — 'the relationships between print symbol and sound patterns' (*English in the National Curriculum*, DFE, 1995).

Plural — a word that indicates 'more than one', for example 'babies'.

Polysyllabic — a word that has more than one syllable, such as 'alligator'.

Prefix — an affix at the beginning of a word, for example '<u>dis</u>appoint', '<u>un</u>happy', '<u>mis</u>hap', '<u>sub</u>marine'.

Short vowel sound — when the vowel is pronounced as the standard letter sound, for example as in '<u>a</u>pple' (initial sound) or as in 'c<u>a</u>t' (middle sound).

Silent letter — these can occur at the beginning, end or middle of words, for example 'b', 'g', 'gh', 'k'. 'E' is frequently silent at the end of words, for example 'kettl<u>e</u>'. Examples of silent letters include: 'throu<u>gh</u>', 'crum<u>b</u>', '<u>k</u>nee', '<u>w</u>rist', 'ca<u>l</u>m', 'si<u>g</u>n', '<u>p</u>salm'.

Singular — a word that expresses 'one of', for example 'chair'.

Suffix — an affix at the end of a word, for example 'want<u>ed</u>', 'use<u>ful</u>', 'alter<u>ation</u>'.

Syllable — a rhythmic segment of a word, spoken or written, which consists of a combination of vowel(s) plus consonant(s) or consonant(s) plus vowel(s).

Triple consonant — three letter 'blends', for example 'str', 'spr'.

Vowel — 'a', 'e', 'i', 'o', 'u'. The letter 'y' can function as a vowel, as in 'ay', 'ey', 'iy', 'oy', 'uy'. 'Y' also functions as a vowel in unusual words such as 'rhythm'. Vowels can be described as being 'long', as in 'day' or 'mice', or 'short' as in 'have' or 'tip'.

Vowel digraph — a combination of two symbols that represent a sound unlike that of either of the individual letters. Examples of vowel digraphs include: 'ai', 'ay', 'ee', 'ie', 'oa', 'oe', 'au'.

SPELLING AND PHONICS KS2

Photocopiables

The pages in this section can be photocopied for use in the classroom or school which has purchased this book, and do not need to be declared in any return in respect of any photocopying licence.

They comprise a varied selection of both pupil and teacher resources, including pupil worksheets, resource material and record sheets to be completed by the teacher or children. Most of the photocopiable pages are related to individual activities in the book; the name of the activity is indicated at the top of the sheet, together with a page reference indicating where the lesson plan for that activity can be found.

Individual pages are discussed in detail within each lesson plan, accompanied by ideas for adaptation where appropriate – of course, each sheet can be adapted to your own needs and those of your class. Sheets can also be coloured, laminated, mounted on to card, enlarged and so on where appropriate.

Pupil worksheets and record sheets have spaces provided for children's names and for noting the date on which each sheet was used. This means that, if so required, they can be included easily within any pupil assessment portfolio. The record sheets on photocopiable pages 153 to 157 are for the purposes of summative assessment and are intended to be used over time.

What do you know about the alphabet?, see page 14

What do you know about the alphabet?

Name _____ **Date** _____

▲ Write out the alphabet in capital letters. The first letter has been written for you.

A_____

_____

▲ Write out the alphabet in lower case letters. The first letter has been written for you.

a_____

_____

▲ Read this sentence which contains every letter of the alphabet. Look for all the letters and then map them on to the alphabet strip below. The first letter has been done for you:

The quick brown fox jumps over the lazy dog.

a b c d e f g h i j k l m n o p q r s t u v w x y z

▲ There are _____ letters in the alphabet.

The vowels are _____

SPELLING AND PHONICS KS2

What else do you know about the alphabet?

Name _____   Date _____

▲ The letter 'm' comes in the middle of the alphabet. Write all the letters which come before it and after it:

_____m_____

▲ Which letter comes before?

_____d   _____k   _____r   _____v

▲ Which letter comes after?

g_____   m_____   q_____   t_____

▲ Look at the letters below. Decide whether they come near to the beginning, middle or end of the alphabet. List each one under one of the headings below:

z q t b e o v m d p a w l c

Beginning	Middle	End

SPELLING AND PHONICS KS2

All the words I can spell: alphabet sheet

Name _____   **Date** _____

▲ Use this sheet *first* before you write your list of words into your dictionary.
You need your 'All the words I can spell' list.
Look at the first letter of each word on the list and copy the word next to the
right letter of the alphabet. Remember, all the words must be written on this list.
When you have finished, check for spellings.

A _____

B _____

C _____

D _____

E _____

F _____

G _____

H _____

I _____

J _____

K _____

L _____

M _____

N _____

O _____

P _____

Q _____

R _____

S _____

T _____

U _____

V _____

W _____

X _____

Y _____

Z _____

**SPELLING AND
PHONICS KS2**

Which word comes first?

Name _____ . Date _____

▲ Look at the words you have written on the alphabet sheet. Does any letter have more than one word written next to it? If so, write the words below in a list. Use a pencil. Write the first letter of the set of words in the box provided:

This set of words starts with the letter ⬭

Draw a line in **red** felt-tipped pen under the second letter.

Draw a line in **blue** felt-tipped pen under the second letter.

Draw a line in **green** felt-tipped pen under the second letter.

Draw a line in **yellow** felt-tipped pen under the second letter.

▲ Look at the alphabet below and mark the second letters on it. Use coloured counters that match the words to do this.

A	B	C	D	E	F	G	H	I	J	K	L	M
N	O	P	Q	R	S	T	U	V	W	X	Y	Z

You can now write the words in alphabetical order. The first word on the list will be the word which has a counter nearest to the letter 'A'.

This set of words starts with the letter ⬭

▲ Now write the list in the correct order into your dictionary.

SPELLING AND PHONICS KS2

Finding out about vowels and consonants

Name _____   **Date** _____

You need: a pencil, two different-coloured felt-tipped pens and a dictionary or alphabet book.

▲ Look at the alphabet at the bottom of the page. Use one of the felt-tipped pens to underline all the vowels.

▲ Write your *full* name here:

Underline *all* the vowels in your name.

My name has _____ consonants.

My name has _____ vowels.

My first name starts with a _____

My middle name starts with a _____

My surname starts with a _____

▲ Write five words that start with a vowel:

_____ _____ _____ _____ _____

▲ Write five words that start with a consonant:

_____ _____ _____ _____ _____

ABCDEFGHIJKLMNOPQRSTUVWXYZ

SPELLING AND PHONICS KS2

Using vowels and consonants

Name _____   Date _____

You need: a pencil, two different-coloured felt-tipped pens and a dictionary.

▲ Write your full name below and underline all the vowels.

How many vowels occur in *each* name?_____

Which vowel(s) occurs most frequently in your name?_____

▲ Look at this list of words: **good   read   feet   soap**

What do you notice about the consonants? Write your ideas below:

_____

What do you notice about the vowels? Write your ideas below:

_____

▲ Write five words that start with a vowel and end with a vowel. Use your dictionary to help you. Write your list below:

_____   _____   _____   _____   _____

▲ Write five words that have two consonants together in the middle. Use your dictionary to help you. Write your list below:

_____   _____   _____   _____   _____

ABCDEFGHIJKLMNOPQRSTUVWXYZ

SPELLING AND
PHONICS KS2

Vowels: working with long 'a' and short 'a'

Name _____ Date _____

Here is the alphabet. Use a felt-tipped pen to underline all the letters which are vowels.

A B C D E F G H I J K L M N O P Q R S T U V W X Y Z

▲ Read the list of words. Underline all the words which have a short 'a' vowel sound in them. The first word has been done to help you.

<u>cat</u>   lane   apple   lake   banner

▲ Read the list of words. Underline all the words which have a long 'a' vowel sound in them. The first word has been done to help you.

<u>sale</u>   apricot   ant   name   astronaut

▲ Make a list of some more words that have a short 'a' in them.

_____ _____ _____ _____

▲ Make a list of some more words that have a long 'a' in them:

_____ _____ _____ _____

Use a dictionary to help you.

SPELLING AND PHONICS KS2

Photocopiables

From word bank to dictionary, see page 25

Word bank on Victorians

Victoria	Albert	German	Queen
Prince	Princess	Consort	penny
Empire	India	poverty	Dickens
Ironbridge	industry	education	London
clothes	carriages	steam	trains
jubilee	mourning	century	nineteenth
sentimentality	cruelty	wealth	families

SPELLING AND
PHONICS KS2

Find that letter: how did you do?

Name _____ Date _____

▲ Use this sheet as you play the game to note how you got on.

Suggestions for what you could write: It was hard/easy, couldn't find right page, lost my place, I was too slow.

Team members' names: _____   _____

Write the letter below:	Write your comments:	
	😃 We did well	🙁 We had problems

SPELLING AND PHONICS KS2

Find that word: how did you do?

Name _____   Date _____

▲ Use this sheet as you play the game to note how you got on.

Suggestions for what you could write: hard, easy, couldn't find letter, lost my place, not sure.

Team members' names: _____   _____

Write the word below:	Write your comments:	
	☺ We did well	☹ We had problems

SPELLING AND PHONICS KS2

Find that headword, see page 34

Do these words belong?

Name _____ Date _____

▲ This is a page from a dictionary. It has two headwords at the top of the page. The headwords represent the first and last words that appear on this particular page. The list of words at the bottom of the page is in a terrible muddle. Some words should not appear on the page at all. Sort the words out into alphabetical order and write them on the page. Cross out the words that should not be on this page.

bag	beaver

bear	tree	band	coat	bean	bank	battle
sand	beach	ball	badger	bag	beaver	baker

SPELLING AND PHONICS KS2

Page from a dictionary

Name _____   **Date** _____

▲ This is a page from a class dictionary on World War Two. At the top of the page is a pair of headwords. Look at the list of words below and decide which words should be written on this page of the dictionary. Sort them into alphabetical order and write them on the page. Look carefully at the second letters of the words to help you sort out the order. Watch out! One of the words listed needs to be crossed out because it doesn't belong on this page.

battle	Churchill

blitz   battle   Churchill   bomb   brigadier   Hitler

SPELLING AND PHONICS KS2

Barely bear!, see page 40

A humorous homophone story

Bernie the bear went to see the sea. Barely had the bear arrived when he went to buy two buckets and spades.

'Oh, that was a bit expensive,' said Bernie, holding his change in his paw. 'I feel quite poor now and I don't think I can buy an ice-cream.'

Just then, his friends Katie and Alice came by with their picnic box. 'What have you got in there?' asked the hungry Bernie.

'Just a pair of pears,' laughed the girls.

All three friends sat on a wooden bench. 'Would you like to share our pears?' asked Katie and Alice.

'I don't know,' said Bernie. 'Well... it would be rude to say no!'

SPELLING AND PHONICS KS2

An exploration of rhyme and alliteration, see page 42

The Pelican Chorus

Name _____   **Date** _____

▲ Read the poem below called 'The Pelican Chorus'. Use a pencil and ruler to underline all the rhyming words in the poem. Two have been done to help you.

The Pelican Chorus
by Edward Lear

King and Queen of the Pelicans <u>we</u>;
No other Birds so grand we <u>see</u>!
None but we have (feet) like (fins)!
With lovely leathery throats and chins!
   Puffskin, Pluffskin, Pelican jee!
   We think no Birds so happy as we!
Plumpskin, Ploshkin, Pelican jill!
We think so then, and we thought so still!

▲ Now go back and read the poem again. This time put a circle round all the alliterative words. (Remember, alliterative words often start with the same letter.) Two have been done to help you.

SPELLING AND
PHONICS KS2

An exploration of rhyme and alliteration, see page 42

Fill in the blanks

Name _____ Date _____

The _____ Chorus

by _____

King and Queen of the _____ we;

No other _____ so grand we see!

None but we have _____ like _____!

With _____ _____ _____

and _____!

_____, _____, _____ jee!

We think no _____ so happy as we!

_____, _____ jill!

We think so then, and we thought so still!

SPELLING AND PHONICS KS2

Exploring spelling families, see page 47

Spelling families

Name _____ Date _____

▲ With your partner, look at this list of words that rhyme with 'Spain' and 'aeroplane'. Decide which part of each word is the rhyme. Using a pencil and ruler, underline the rhymes:

Spain	pain	main	rain
aeroplane	mane	pane	crane
reign	explain	remain	lane
Shane	slain		

▲ How many different ways is the rhyme at the end of the words spelled?

▲ Can you sort the list into spelling families? Rewrite the list in the space below, splitting the words into their separate families. (It might help to use different-coloured felt-tipped pens to identify the words.)

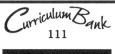

SPELLING AND PHONICS KS2

Exploring spelling families, see page 47

Working with rhyme

Name _____   **Date** _____

▲ First read the poem. Then pick a pair of rhymes from the poem and write them down. Next make a list of all the words you can think of that rhyme with the pair of rhyming words. Use a dictionary to help you.

▲ Look at the words carefully and then sort the words out into spelling families. Write the families below.

▲ Are any of the words homophones? If so, write them down below. Can you write a definition for each homophone to explain the difference in their meaning?

SPELLING AND PHONICS KS2

Writing limericks: the spelling of sounds, see page 52

My limerick: what rhymes with...?

Name _____ Date _____

To write a limerick you need to write *five* lines of poetry. The first line of the poem should be about a person and a place, for example:

> '*There was a young man from Southend*'

Line 2 of the poem rhymes with line 1.

Line 3 of the poem ends in a *new* rhyme.

Line 4 of the poem rhymes with line 3.

The last line should rhyme with the *first two* lines.

To write your limerick, you need to think 'What rhymes with...?'

▲ Write your ideas here:

Rhymes for lines 1, 2 and 5	Rhymes for lines 3 and 4
_____	_____
_____	_____
_____	_____
_____	_____
_____	_____

SPELLING AND PHONICS KS2

What makes them different?

Name _____ Date _____

▲ First, take turns to read your limerick to your partner.

▲ Choose *one* of the limericks and make a list of all the rhyming words in the poem:

Rhymes from lines 1, 2 and 5	Rhymes from lines 3 and 4
_____	_____
_____	_____
_____	_____
_____	_____

▲ What do you notice about the spelling of the rhymes in lines 1, 2 and 5? Make some notes:

_____

_____

_____

▲ Can you think of some other words that share the same rhyme as lines 1, 2 and 5? Make a list:

_____

_____

_____

SPELLING AND PHONICS KS2

The old joke book, see page 55

Starter jokes (1)

Q. Why are plum stones like milestones?
A. They are never found in pears (pairs).

Q. What is the most important part of a lion?
A. The main (mane) part.

Q. Which side of a round cake is the left side?
A. The side which isn't eaten.

Q. Why is it against the law to whisper?
A. Because it isn't allowed (aloud).

Q. When is water like a kangaroo?
A. When it makes a spring.

Q. When do grapes make the news?
A. When they are in the press.

Q. Which vegetable should never be put in a saucepan?
A. Leeks (leaks).

Q. Why should a sailor know where King Neptune lives?
A. Because he's been to see (sea).

Q. What tradesman is lazy?
A. A baker because he's a loafer.

Q. How do you make eleven an even number?
A. Remove the first two letters (even).

Q. When is a magazine like a sick person?
A. When it's weakly (weekly).

Q. From which six-letter word can you remove three letters and leave one?
A. Throne (t, h, r – one).

SPELLING AND PHONICS KS2

Photocopiables

The old joke book, see page 55

Starter jokes (2)

Q. Where will you find two trees?
A. Where there are pear (pair) trees.

Q. Why should you never tell a secret to a peacock?
A. Because they're always spreading tales (tails).

Q. Why did the deaf woman ask for a letter A?
A. Because it made 'her' hear.

Q. Why is a fog like a lost boy?
A. Because they are both missed (mist).

Q. When do you feel like the wheel of a bicycle?
A. At night when you're tired (tyred).

Q. Why will a dustman never accept an invitation?
A. Because he's a refuse man.

Q. What did the flour say to the water?
A. We'll be needed (kneaded) to make dough.

Q. Why did the farmer give the pig a collar?
A. To go with his pig's tie (pigsty).

Q. What makes men mean?
A. The letter A.

Q. When is a cow not a cow?
A. When it is led (lead).

Q. When did only three vowels exist?
A. Before U and I were born.

Q. Why are jockeys like clouds?
A. Because they both hold the rains (reins).

Q. Where did Noah keep his bees?
A. In the archives (ark hives).

Negative prefixes, see page 59

Negative prefixes cards

mis-	dis-	
take	lead	agree
qualify	approve	pleasure
satisfaction	service	solve
similar	appear	appoint
hear	direct	behave
trust	laid	fortune
place	interested	believe
read	honest	like

SPELLING AND
PHONICS KS2

Negative prefixes, see page 59

Negative prefixes: sorting sheet

Name _____   Date _____

▲ To play this game you will need a partner and a set of negative prefixes cards. Take out the prefixes 'mis-' and 'dis-'. Now try each of the words with each of the prefixes. When you think you have made a real word, write it down on the chart below.

Word	Prefix + word	Meaning of the new word

▲ These words will go with both prefixes:

SPELLING AND PHONICS KS2

Prefix pairs, see page 61

Prefix pairs (1)

Prefix	Meaning
ante	before
anti	against
bi	two
cent	hundred
chromo	colour
circum	around
co	together/jointly
contra	against
counter	against
demi	half
fore	in front/beforehand
hemi	half
hydro	water
hyper	too much
hypo	too little
inter	between
intra	within

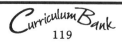

Prefix pairs (2)

Prefix	Meaning
mal	bad
manu	hand
mega	large
micro	small
mono	one
multi	many
no	not
non	not
omni	all
photo	light
poly	many/much
pseudo	false
retro	backwards
semi	half
sub	under
super	above
ultra	extreme

SPELLING AND
PHONICS KS2

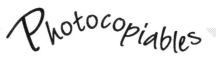
Template for prefix hexagon

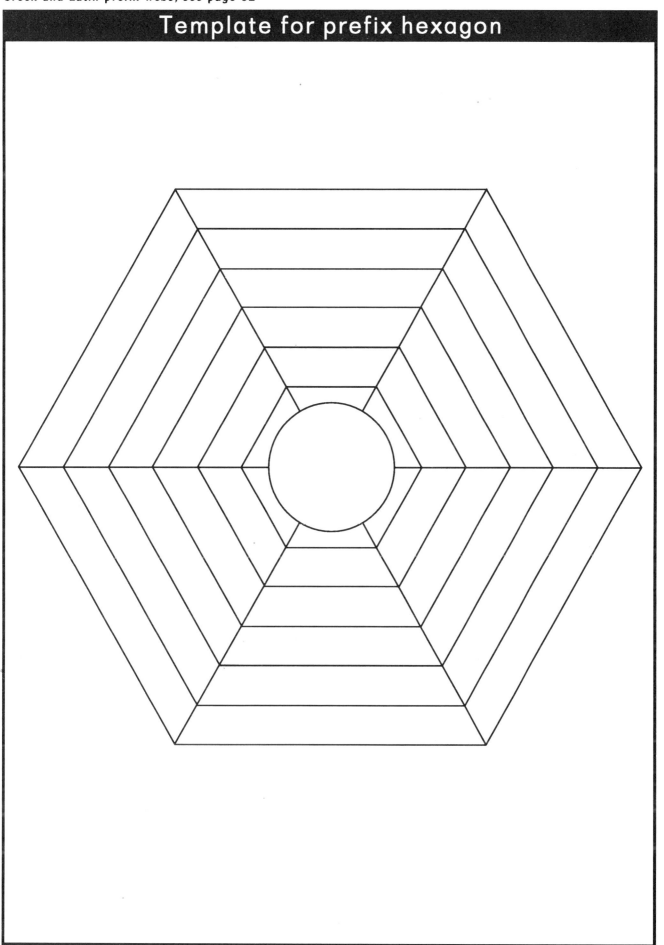

**SPELLING AND
PHONICS KS2**

Suffix rules!, see page 65

Rule cards for the game

1 When a suffix is added to a word which ends in a consonant followed by the letter 'y', the 'y' must be changed to 'i'.
Example: 'happy' + '-ness' = 'happiness'.
If the 'y' has a vowel before it, it does not change to 'i'. *Example:* 'play' + '-ful' = 'playful'.

2 When it is used as a suffix, 'full' loses an 'l' and is written as '-ful'. *Example:* 'hope' + 'full' (meaning 'full of hope') = 'hopeful'.

3 When '-ful' becomes '-fully', the 'ly' ending is added to '-ful' to make '-fully', so there are two 'l's again. *Example:* 'beautiful' + 'ly' = 'beautifully'.

4 If the last letter of the root word is the same as the first letter of the suffix, both letters remain so that there is a double consonant.
Example: 'clean' + '-ness' = 'cleanness'.

5 If the root word ends in an 'e' no change is needed; the suffix is added to the whole word.
Example: 'peace' + '-ful' = 'peaceful'.

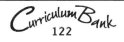

Suffix rules!, see page 65

Record of new words made (-ful -fully -ness -less)

Name _____   Date _____

Root word	Suffix	New word
beauty	-ful	beautiful
beauty	-fully	beautifully

▲ Look at the examples above and write down the words you have made in the same way. Remember to check the rules about the spelling.

Root word	Suffix	New word

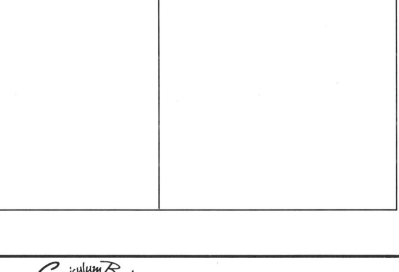

Suffix rules!, see page 65

Root word cards

peace	play	pity	truth
pain	faith	mercy	shame
use	care	sudden	keen
love	empty	plenty	weary
ugly	duty	cheer	thank
wonder	help	power	spite
delight	disgrace	forget	hope
faith	mean	weak	cheap
clever	bold	dark	soft
wild	dirty	noisy	silly
funny	cold	messy	busy
great	fresh	thick	quiet
quick	close	point	colour
rest	end	fear	small
worth	wish	wake	doubt
flavour	harm	icy	joy
kind	mind	right	sorrow

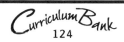

Kim's game, see page 66

Vowel digraph cards

oe	ui	ue	ie
does	juice	fuel	pie
goes	fruit	duel	die
shoes	guilt	hue	field
toes	guitar	due	believe
echoes	guinea-pig	guess	chief
heroes	guide	sue	lie
volcanoes	guild	suet	niece
potatoes	nuisance	blue	piece
tomatoes	penguin	fatigue	shield
poem	ruin	vague	thief
poetry	genuine	league	priest
roe	quite	rogue	fierce
poet	squirrel	duet	cashier
hoe	suit	cruel	yield

SPELLING AND
PHONICS KS2

Word detectives, see page 68

Timeline for the English language

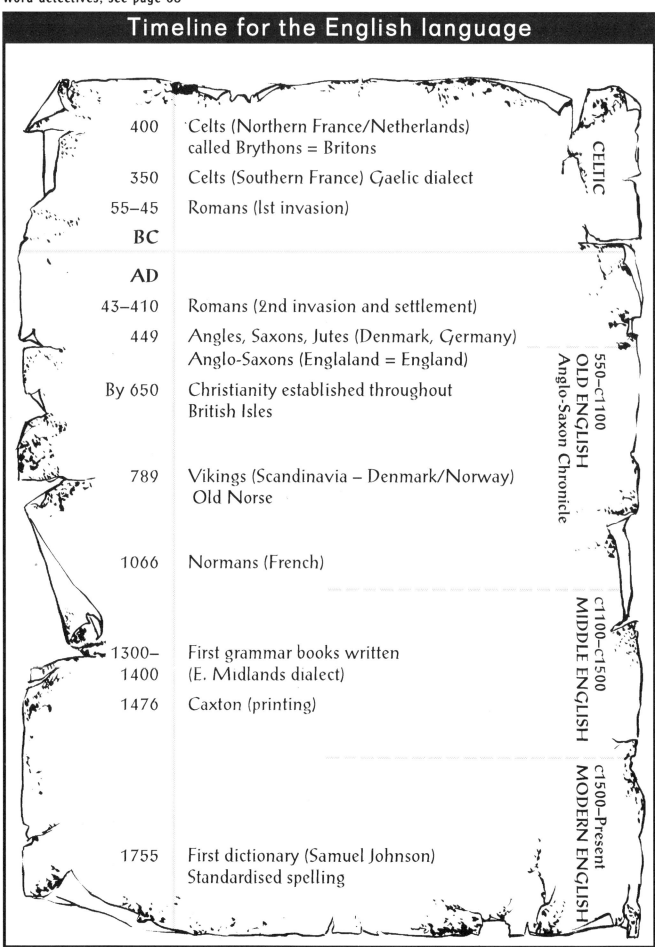

BC		CELTIC
400	Celts (Northern France/Netherlands) called Brythons = Britons	
350	Celts (Southern France) Gaelic dialect	
55–45	Romans (1st invasion)	

AD		
43–410	Romans (2nd invasion and settlement)	
449	Angles, Saxons, Jutes (Denmark, Germany) Anglo-Saxons (Englaland = England)	550–c1100 OLD ENGLISH Anglo-Saxon Chronicle
By 650	Christianity established throughout British Isles	
789	Vikings (Scandinavia – Denmark/Norway) Old Norse	
1066	Normans (French)	
1300–1400	First grammar books written (E. Midlands dialect)	c1100–c1500 MIDDLE ENGLISH
1476	Caxton (printing)	
1755	First dictionary (Samuel Johnson) Standardised spelling	c1500–Present MODERN ENGLISH

SPELLING AND
PHONICS KS2

Celtic place-names

Name _____ **Date** _____

▲ The Celtic Britons gave us words for many features of the countryside. These can still be found in place-names in the British Isles. Look at a map of Britain and try to find some place-names which have these Celtic words in them.

mor – sea
caer/car – fortress
dun – fort
tor – hill
bal – homestead/hamlet
aber – mouth of a river
dun/dum – hill or fort

lan/llan – church
rhos/ros – rough moorland
tre – farm/homestead
pen – hill/head/top
afon/avon – river
cwm/cum/combe – a deep valley

▲ Make a list here of all the place-names you find.

SPELLING AND PHONICS KS2

Old English words

Name _____   **Date** _____

▲ A great many of the words we use in English today have come directly from Old English. Have a look at this list and see if you can write the modern spelling by the side of each word. You can check your guesses by looking up the modern word in a dictionary to see what word it comes from.

Old English	Modern English
aefter	
aet	
eall	
butan	
beforan	
behindan	
haefde	
bi	
hwaet?	
hwy?	
ofer	
uppan	
writan	
beon	
eow	
waes	
thaet	

▲ If you find it hard to guess, say the word out loud and see if it sounds like a word you know.

Double consonant wordsearch, see page 72

Wordsearch

Name _____   Date _____

butter		T	I	L	M	L	A	D	D	L
cattle		O	W	B	M	I	D	D	L	E
better		M	C	U	H	A	Y	B	C	S
middle		O	R	T	T	J	P	P	S	S
dinner		R	R	T	M	L	A	O	K	O
rabbit		R	C	E	W	O	R	R	Y	N
grass		O	R	R	S	T	R	R	E	Y
parrot		W	B	D	C	U	O	M	L	Q
worry		W	O	N	A	T	T	P	L	V
follow		X	R	M	T	P	Z	P	O	Y
yellow		A	R	U	T	P	P	I	W	L
borrow		F	O	L	L	O	W	L	E	B
lesson		R	W	B	E	F	C	L	E	E
tomorrow		D	A	P	R	F	G	O	S	T
apple		H	J	B	Q	E	M	W	P	T
offer		Q	T	W	B	R	U	S	R	E
pillow		B	F	W	D	I	N	N	E	R
		G	R	A	S	S	T	V	B	F

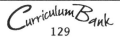
SPELLING AND PHONICS KS2

Plurals puzzle, see page 73

Nouns ending in 'y' cards

spy	key	lady	alley
baby	cry	tray	toy
story	storey	penny	ferry
jelly	abbey	puppy	lorry
library	journey	family	chimney
fly	strawberry	donkey	diary
dairy	quay	melody	monkey
party	holiday	enemy	birthday
monastery	turkey	quarry	allergy
jersey	display	fairy	berry
buoy	estuary	alloy	essay
territory	trolley	kidney	volley
railway	cowboy	valley	city
pony	body	hobby	cherry
discovery	mystery	factory	aunty

SPELLING AND
PHONICS KS2

Apostrophe lotto cards (1)

cannot	had not	have not
do not	has not	need not
will not	was not	were not
is not	shall not	would not
are not	does not	should not
did not	must not	could not
he is	that is	I will
he has	what is	I shall
she is	here is	we will
she has	there is	we shall
who is	I am	he will

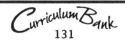

SPELLING AND PHONICS KS2

Apostrophe lotto, see page 74

Apostrophe lotto cards (2)

he shall	you will	who shall
she will	you shall	they will
she shall	who will	they shall
I had	you would	we are
I would	who had	you are
he had	who would	who are
he would	I have	they are
we had	you have	we have
we would	they had	they have
you had	they would	

**SPELLING AND
PHONICS KS2**

Apostrophe lotto, see page 74

Template for board

<table>
<tr><td></td><td></td><td></td><td></td></tr>
<tr><td></td><td></td><td></td><td></td></tr>
<tr><td></td><td></td><td></td><td></td></tr>
<tr><td></td><td></td><td></td><td></td></tr>
</table>

Apostrophe lotto, see page 74

Belonging apostrophes

Name _____   **Date** _____

▲ As well as being used to show that letters have been missed out of words (as in 'didn't', where the apostrophe shows that the letter 'o' is missed out), the apostrophe can also be used to show that something belongs to someone or something.
Look at these examples:

'This is the girl's bicycle' *means*
'This is the bicycle belonging to the girl.'
'He has his father's hat' *means*
'He has the hat belonging to his father.'

▲ Another way of checking whether an apostrophe should be there is to put in 'his', 'her', 'their' or 'its', and see if it makes sense. For example:

'my mother's book' – Could you say:
'my mother, her book'? – Yes, it makes sense.
'the school's entrance' – Could you say:
'the school, its entrance'? – Yes, it makes sense.

▲ Now try these yourself. Put in the apostrophe in the word which is underlined, *if there should be one.*

1. I have just finished reading my <u>brothers</u> book.
2. The teacher asked me to pick up all the <u>childrens</u> pencils.
3. I have eaten all my Easter <u>eggs</u>.
4. The <u>boys</u> were all keen to play football in the park.
5. I wonder what happened to that <u>boys</u> football?
6. Two <u>boys</u> were cleaning out the <u>teachers</u> cupboard.
7. When my <u>friends</u> came to play, we borrowed my <u>sisters</u> CD-player.
8. A <u>girls</u> coat and a <u>boys</u> scarf were found in the playground.
9. On <u>Saturdays</u> I take my baby <u>brothers</u> <u>books</u> back to the library.

SPELLING AND PHONICS KS2

Knight's knowledge, see page 76

Silent 'k' word bank

knack	kneel	knocker
knapsack	knell	knoll
knave	knight	knot
knee	knit	know
knife	knob	knowledge
knead	knock	knuckles

Knight's knowledge, see page 76

Knight's knowledge board

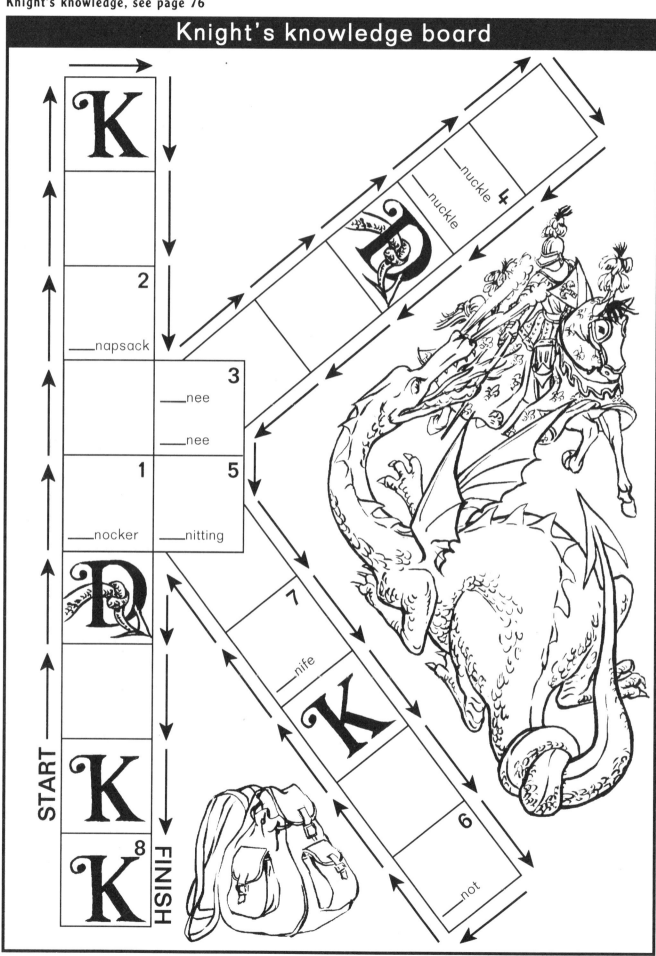

K

2

___napsack

3

___nee

___nee

1

___nocker

5

___nitting

D

___nuckle

___nuckle

4

7

___nife

K

6

___not

D

START

K

FINISH

K 8

Knight's knowledge, see page 76

Letter 'k' resource bank

K	K	K	K	K	K	K	K	K	K	K	K
K	K	K	K	K	K	K	K	K	K	K	K
K	K	K	K	K	K	K	K	K	K	K	K
K	K	K	K	K	K	K	K	K	K	K	K
K	K	K	K	K	K	K	K	K	K	K	K
K	K	K	K	K	K	K	K	K	K	K	K
K	K	K	K	K	K	K	K	K	K	K	K
K	K	K	K	K	K	K	K	K	K	K	K
K	K	K	K	K	K	K	K	K	K	K	K
K	K	K	K	K	K	K	K	K	K	K	K
K	K	K	K	K	K	K	K	K	K	K	K
K	K	K	K	K	K	K	K	K	K	K	K
K	K	K	K	K	K	K	K	K	K	K	K
K	K	K	K	K	K	K	K	K	K	K	K
K	K	K	K	K	K	K	K	K	K	K	K

SPELLING AND
PHONICS KS2

Knight's knowledge, see page 76

Knight's knowledge cards

1. Bang on the door. Knock! knock! knock! Give the knocker a 'k' and the door will unlock!

2. Here is a knapsack but it needs a 'k'. If you give it one you can go on your way.

3. This passage is low. It's a tight squeeze. Leave two 'k's behind for both of your knees.

4. Your knuckles are sore. You feel sad. Leave two 'k's behind and it won't be so bad!

5. The king is knitting his winter vest. Give him a 'k' and he'll take a rest.

6. The dragon is sleeping and snoring a lot. Drop a 'k' and untie his knot.

7. Look by the stone and you'll find the knife. Leave your last 'k' and run for your life.

8. Now the knave has his knife and has gone on his way. And you have the knowledge about silent 'k'!

Knight's knowledge, see page 76

Knight's knowledge: the rules (1)

The object of the game
To move your token round the board, leaving silent 'k's on all the numbered squares. The first player to reach square number 8 and read their last 'Knight's knowledge card' is the winner.

Each player needs:
▲ a 'Knight's knowledge' game board;
▲ a token (a knight or a coloured counter);
▲ a pack of eight 'Knight's knowledge cards' sorted into the correct order;
▲ a bag of eight 'k's.

The players share:
▲ a dice;
▲ a box of spare 'k's.

What you need to know about the board:
▲ The board is in the shape of a 'k'.
▲ The arrows indicate how the tokens should move around the board.
▲ There is a start square and a finish square.
▲ During the game the token visits every square twice.
▲ There are eight 'Knight's knowledge' squares. Each one has a number on it which matches the eight 'Knight's knowledge cards'.
▲ Each 'Knight's knowledge' square has a silent 'k' word on it but the silent 'k's are missing.
▲ There are two silent 'k' squares, marked by a large 'K'. These are lucky to land on (see rule 7).
▲ There are two 'Dragon's knot' squares, marked by a large 'D'. These are unlucky to land on (see rule 6).

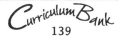
SPELLING AND
PHONICS KS2

Knight's knowledge: the rules (2)

The rules

1. Place your knight on the 'Start' square.
2. You can throw any number to start.
3. The aim is to land on each of the numbered 'Knight's knowledge' squares.
4. If you throw the right number and land on a 'Knight's knowledge' square pick up a 'Knight's knowledge card' with a matching number. The card will tell you what to do. For example, when you land on square number 1 the card tells you to give the word '...nocker' a silent 'k'. Take a silent 'k' from your bag and put it in the correct place.
5. If you miss a 'Knight's knowledge' square, on your next throw you can move back to the square if you throw exactly the right number.
6. If you are unfortunate enough to land on a 'Dragon's knot' square marked by a giant 'D' you have to pay a penalty. A 'k' that you have already put down on a word must be removed from the board and goes back into your bag. You will have to try the word again later.
7. If you land on a 'Silent k' square you have a free turn and can immediately put a 'k' on to any word that needs one.
8. If you run out of 'k's miss a turn and take a spare 'k' from the spare 'k' box.
9. If you go all the way round the board, reach the finish and still have not landed on all the 'Knight's knowledge squares', a penalty point will be counted for each square missed. If one of your opponents goes round the board and leaves a silent 'k' on each of the 'Knight's knowledge squares' then he will be the winner.
10. The winner is the first person to reach square number 8, having left silent 'k' cards on all the 'Knight's knowledge' squares on the way. Don't forget to read the last 'Knight's knowledge card'.

Good luck!

Knight's knowledge sheet (1)

Name _____ **Date** _____

▲ On the lines below, write down six silent 'k' words. Try to spell the words from memory.

▲ Now use a dictionary or the class word bank to check your spellings. If you spelled a word incorrectly use the 'look–cover–write–check' method to help you memorise the word. When you are ready, write the word again below.

▲ Write down a simple rule that will help other people remember how to spell words with a silent 'k'.

**SPELLING AND
PHONICS KS2**

Knight's knowledge, see page 76

Knight's knowledge sheet (2)

Name _____   **Date** _____

▲ In the boxes below, draw three things that start with silent 'k'. Write their names underneath. Use the class word bank to help you.

_____   _____   _____

▲ What is the second letter in all the silent 'k' words?

The second letter is _____

▲ Choose two silent 'k' words and try to learn the spellings. Use the 'look–cover–write–check' system to help you. When you think you know the spellings write the words below.

_____   _____

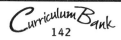

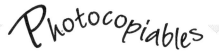

The floating 'h', see page 78

The Haunted House

Name _____   **Date** _____

▲ The scribe who has written this page has got into a terrible muddle because he doesn't know that English spelling has changed in the last 600 years. He has used the spelling he knows for some of the words. Can you correct all the underlined words that have 'wh' or 'gh' in them, so that they are spelled as they should be in the 1990s? To help you put the scribe's mistakes right, the modern spellings of the words are at the bottom of the page. You have to decide which one is which and write the correct words in the spaces above the underlined words.

The three children went quietly up the steps to the house. They were all a little <u>frihtened</u> because it was the middle of the <u>niht</u> and they didn't know what they would find behind the big front door.

Ranjit, <u>hwa</u> was the eldest, <u>thoht</u> that they should all go home and wait until it was <u>liht</u> before they went in to look for the <u>gost</u>. The other two said they <u>miht</u> as well go on now they were here, because they didn't think they would be brave <u>enouh</u> to come back the next <u>niht</u>. As they pushed open the door on its rusty hinges each of them <u>thoht</u> about <u>hwaet</u> they would find. They wondered <u>hwaether</u> the stories they had heard could possibly be true. They expected some <u>gastly</u> <u>siht</u> to meet their eyes.

'<u>Hwaet</u> was that!' shouted Danny. 'I <u>thoht</u> I saw something moving.'

'It was only a bat,' said Lisa. '<u>Hwaenne</u> you disturb them, they fly around looking for a new place to hang about!'

'We can do without your silly jokes,' Ranjit snapped.

Now they were all very nervous and sure that <u>hwaet</u> they would see next would be the <u>gost</u>. Danny was wondering <u>hwy</u> he had agreed to come on this daft adventure. Suddenly there was a very loud, wailing scream. In their panic, they ran... and ran... <u>riht</u> out of the house. They didn't stop until they reached the safety of the <u>lihts</u> in the street.

'I'm never going <u>gost</u> hunting again!' panted Danny. And the others agreed.

<u>Hwaet</u> they didn't know was that their <u>gost</u> was only a stray cat <u>hwa</u> was as

frightened	night	light/lights	sight	might	thought	right
when	who	why	what	whether	ghost	ghastly	enough

143

SPELLING AND PHONICS KS2

Hard 'c' and soft 'c'

Name _____   Date _____

▲ All these words have a 'c' at the beginning. Can you sort the words into the hard 'c' set and the soft 'c' set? The first words have been done for you.

cart	centigrade	camera
certificate	ceiling	circle
carpet	Centurian	computer
century	castle	caterpillar

The hard 'c' set	The soft 'c' set
corner	cell

▲ There is something interesting about the 'c' sound in the words 'concentrate' and 'concert'. Say the words aloud carefully and write down what you have found out.

Hard and soft consonants, see page 80

Hard and soft 'c' word bank

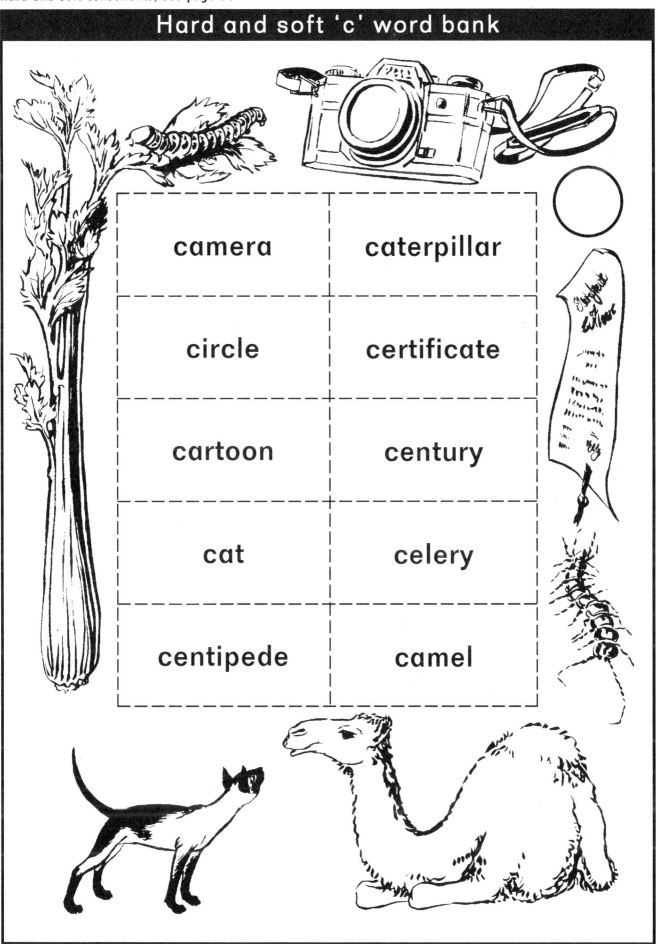

camera	caterpillar
circle	certificate
cartoon	century
cat	celery
centipede	camel

SPELLING AND PHONICS KS2

Silent 'b' crossword (1)

Name _____   **Date** _____

Clues Across

1 You have one on each hand (5)

2 Little bits of bread (6)

3 Arms and legs are called.... (5)

4 This explodes (4)

5 When you owe someone money (4)

6 You tidy your hair with this (4)

Clues Down

2 You do this to reach the top (5)

5 Someone who cannot speak (4)

7 When you are not sure about something (8)

8 When it's very cold and your fingers feel dead (4)

9 A young sheep (4)

10 Not obvious, rhymes with 'shuttle' (6)

11 A pharoah, a queen or a prince might be buried in this (4)

Notes

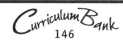
SPELLING AND PHONICS KS2

Silent 'b' crossword (2)

Name _____   **Date** _____

Clues
Across
1 Little bits of bread (6)
2 Arms and legs are called... (5)
3 This explodes (4)

Clues Down
2 A young sheep (4)
4 You have one on each hand (5)
5 When it's cold and your fingers feel dead (4)

Notes

SPELLING AND PHONICS KS2

Silent 'b' crossword (3)

Name _____   **Date** _____

Clues Across
1. You have one on each hand (5)
2. Little bits of bread (6)
3. Arms and legs are called.... (5)
4. This explodes (4)
5. When you owe someone money (4)
6. You tidy your hair with this (4)

Clues Down
2 You do this to reach the top (5)
5 Someone who cannot speak (4)
7 When you are not sure about something (8)
8 When it's very cold and your fingers feel dead (4)
9 A young sheep (4)
10 Not obvious, rhymes with 'shuttle' (6)
11 A pharoah, a queen or a prince might be buried in this (4)

Notes

Don't blame Mulcaster, see page 85

Long-vowel silent 'e' (1)

Name _____   Date _____

▲ Here are some silent 'e' words that have 'a' in them.

ace	fade	age	bake
name	ape	case	crate

Look at your list. Can you think of some other silent 'e' word families that have 'a' in them?

▲ Here are some silent 'e' words that have 'i' in them.

ice	hide	life	bike
file	dine	pipe	dive

Look at your list. Can you think of some other silent 'e' word families that have 'i' in them?

SPELLING AND PHONICS KS2

Long-vowel silent 'e' (2)

Name _____ Date _____

▲ Here are some silent 'e' words that have 'o' in them.

code	hole	home	bone
hope	nose	dote	cove

Look at your list. Can you think of some other silent 'e' word families that have 'o' in them?

▲ Here are some silent 'e' words that have 'u' in them.

cube	crude	fume	mule
dupe	cure	use	cute

Look at your list. Can you think of some other silent 'e' word families that have 'u' in them?

Fascinating 'sc' crossword, see page 89

Fascinating 'sc' crossword (1)

Name _____ Date _____

Clues Across

1 A person who studies science (9)

2 Another word for interesting (11)

3 Your children's children's children are your... (11)

4 The fishy sign of the zodiac (6)

5 This goes on a stage during a play (7)

6 The Queen held this in her hand at her coronation (7)

Clues Down

1 You cut paper with these (8)

2 Things that glow in the dark are... (11)

7 A follower of Christ (8)

8 An old-fashioned tool for cutting grass (6)

9 Someone who is knocked out (11)

10 Another word for perfume (5)

Notes

**SPELLING AND
PHONICS KS2**

Fascinating 'sc' crossword (2)

Name _____   Date _____

Notes

Alphabet knowledge record sheet

Name:	**Age:**

Date started: **Date finished:**

Languages spoken:

Observations:

Comment below on the child's alphabetic knowledge:

Can recite the alphabet.	
Can write the alphabet.	
Comment on any confusion between upper/lower case letters.	
Can make approximations as to whether letters are at the beginning/middle/end of alphabet.	
If given a letter at random can identify preceding letter(s).	
If given a letter at random can identify following letter(s).	

Other comments:

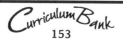
**SPELLING AND
PHONICS KS2**

Vowels and consonants record sheet

Name:	Age:

Date started:	Date finished:

Languages spoken:

Observations:

Comment below on the child's knowledge of vowels and consonants:

Can name the vowels.	
Can name the consonants	
Can use the term 'vowel' when discussing words and spellings.	
Can use the term 'consonant' when discussing words and spellings.	
Has had experience of talking about short vowels.	
Has had experience of talking about long vowels.	

Other comments:

Dictionary skills record sheet

Name:	**Age:**
Date started:	**Date finished:**

✓	**Tick if knowledge demonstrated**	**?**	**if more experience needed**

Knows alphabet order.	☐
Can find location of initial letter in dictionary.	☐
Uses page headings to pinpoint word.	☐
Can use second letter of word to locate words.	☐
Can use subsequent letters to locate words.	☐
Can locate definitions.	☐
Understands abbreviations, word classes (n., adj., adv., conj., prep., pron., v.).	☐
Understands abbreviations, origins (Gk, L, Fr., OE, Eng.).	☐
Is able to use simple/picture dictionary.	☐
Is able to use standard dictionary.	☐
Is able to use dictionary independently to check own spellings.	☐
Is able to use thesaurus.	☐

Other comments:

SPELLING AND PHONICS KS2

Rhyme and alliteration record sheet

Name:	Age:

Date started: — **Date finished:**

Languages spoken:

Observations:

Comment below on the child's awareness of rhyme and alliteration:

Can identify pairs of rhymes when listening to poetry.	
Can identify alliterative words when listening to poetry.	
Can identify the 'odd one out' in a set of rhyming words.	
Can identify the 'odd one out' in a set of alliterative words.	
Can identify words in print that rhyme.	
Can identify alliterative words in print.	
Notices differences in the spellings of some rhyming words.	
Shows sensitivity to half-rhymes.	
Shows evidence of using knowledge of rhyme families in spelling of words.	
Uses knowledge of 'onset' and 'rime' when analysing and spelling words.	

Other comments:

SPELLING AND PHONICS KS2

Homophones record sheet

Name:	**Age:**
Date started:	**Date finished:**
Languages spoken:	
Observations:	

Comment below on the child's knowledge and awareness of homophones:

Child's comments on homophones that they hear: for example, 'There's see and sea.'	
Child's comments on different meanings of pairs of homophones.	
Child's awareness of homophones in their written form.	
Child's effectiveness at making distinctions between pairs of homophones in their spelling.	

Other comments:

SPELLING AND PHONICS KS2

INFORMATION TECHNOLOGY WITHIN SPELLING AND PHONICS

The information technology activities outlined in this book can be used to develop and assess children's IT capability as outlined in the National Curriculum. Types of software rather than names of specific programs have been mentioned to enable teachers to use the ideas regardless of the computers used.

Main IT focus

The main emphasis for the development of IT capability within these activities is on communicating information.

However, in this area of the curriculum there are many software packages which support children's learning in specific activities highlighted in this book. Teachers may still want to use specific software which operates on their computers and which addresses the content and understanding of the subject being taught. Many of the activities in this book have a practical base and give children opportunities to use concrete materials and resources to develop their understanding and use of language. Content specific software should not be used to replace such experiences but to develop or reinforce understanding only after initial practical work. Teachers should also be aware that although such software may assist pupils in developing language skills, it may add little to the development of their pupils' IT capability.

Word processors

During Key Stage 2 pupils will be developing their confidence and competence to use word processing or desktop publishing packages. Many word processors now have basic desktop publishing features and it may be possible to use a single piece of software for most writing tasks. A key difference, however, between the two types of software is the way in which text is placed on the page. In a desktop publishing package text is generally placed inside a frame which can be altered in size and shape, the text automatically being reformatted to fill the new shape. This provides a flexible way for children to organise text on a page and to experiment with different types of layouts and formats.

Children should already have a basic knowledge of the keyboard and should be given opportunities to develop some of the more sophisticated aspects of using a word processor or desktop publishing package. These should include:

Basic skills

▲ the use of more than a single finger/hand when typing, particularly as children become more proficient and know where letters are located;

▲ how to separate and join text using the *return* and *delete* keys;

▲ how to move the cursor to a mistake and correct it, rather than deleting all the text back to the mistake, making the correction and then retyping the deleted text;

▲ how to scroll around the document using the mouse or cursor keys;

▲ how to select an appropriate font from a menu;

▲ how to change the size and/or colour of a font;

▲ how to underline a word or line;

▲ how to alter the style of text, for example italics or bold;

▲ how to centre text using the centre command;

▲ using the Tab key to create columns;

▲ how to fully justify text to line up the right-hand margin and how to reset this option;

▲ how to save and retrieve work from a disk, eventually unaided;

▲ printing their completed work without support from you;

▲ using a spelling checker to check their work.

More advanced skills

▲ altering the 'ruler' to change margins and set Tab keys;

▲ adding page numbers;

▲ setting up a 'master page' to create a consistent layout throughout a document;

▲ setting up a text style to use within a document;

▲ adding a picture to a document, positioning the picture and resizing it.

Points to note

▲ Some children will take a long time to enter text at the keyboard so it is important to ensure that the writing tasks are kept short and that where possible there is other support available to teach and assist the child. Adult helpers can often be used in this way, provided they have the relevant skills and know when to offer guidance. It is important for teachers to be available to intervene, as children are working, to teach them new skills appropriate to the task being undertaken.

▲ Children should be given opportunities to originate their work at the computer keyboard rather than always writing it out longhand and simply using the word processor to make a 'fair copy' for their folder or display purposes. It is often appropriate for a child to make her first draft at the keyboard, save it, print it out and then redraft it away from the keyboard, thus giving another child the opportunity to use the computer. The first child can return at a later time to make any changes that she has decided upon and format the final copy for printing.

▲ Not every child has to undertake every writing suggestion, using the computer, made in this book. You could organise children to undertake different writing tasks over time, some using more conventional written methods and others using the computer. This would also provide an opportunity for you to provide activities at different levels of IT capability and to discuss with the children the relative merits of the use of IT for various purposes.

IT links

The grids on this page relate the activities in this book to specific areas of IT and to relevant software resources. Activities are referenced by page number rather than by name. (Bold page numbers indicate activities which have expanded IT content.) The software listed is a selection of programs generally available to primary schools, and is not intended as a recommended list. The software featured should be available from most good educational software retailers.

AREA OF IT	TYPE OF SOFTWARE	ACTIVITIES (PAGE NOS.)			
		CHAPTER 1	CHAPTER 2	CHAPTER 3	CHAPTER 4
Communicating Information	Word Processing/DTP	16, **18**, 20, 22, 25	40, **42**, 44, 47, 50, 52, 55	58, 59, 61, 62, 68	**72**, 80, 85
Communicating Information	Talking Word Processor	22	42		
Communicating Information	Art/graphics	25, 37	40, 44		72
Communicating Information	Framework				
Communicating Information	CD-ROM	22, 25	40, 44		
Communicating Information	Multimedia Activities		**55**		**80**

SOFTWARE TYPE	BBC/MASTER	RISCOS	NIMBUS/186	WINDOWS	MACINTOSH
Word Processor	*Stylus* *Folio* *Prompt/Writer*	*Phases* *Pendown 2* *Desk Top Folio*	*All Write* *Write On*	*My Word* *Kid Works 2* *Creative Writer*	*Kid Works 2* *EasyWorks* *Creative Writer*
Desk Top Publisher	*Front Page Extra* *Typesetter*	*Desk Top Folio* *First Page* *Front Page Extra* *Impression Style*	*Front Page Extra* *NewSPAper*	*Creative Writer* *NewSPAper*	*Creative Writer*
		Ovation			
Art/Graphics	*Picture Builder* *Image* *Kid Pix*	*1st Paint* *Revelation* *Splash*	*Picture Builder* *PaintSpa*	*Colour Magic* *Kid Pix 2*	*Kid Pix 2*
Multimedia Authoring	*Key Author*	*Magpie* *Genesis*		*MMBox2* *Genesis*	*HyperStudio*

SPELLING AND PHONICS KS2

	MATHS	SCIENCE	GEOGRAPHY AND HISTORY	ART	D & T	MUSIC
ALPHABETIC AND DICTIONARY KNOWLEDGE	Symmetry and asymmetry of letters. Designing symmetrical crossword grids. Graphs, eg. timed dictionary games.	Sounds: making sounds; vibration; materials which conduct sound. Classification of animals and plants.	Chronology, timelines. History of Roman alphabet, history of dictionaries. Place-names in Britain (word bank). Word banks relating to different history topics.	Designing and making alphabet friezes. Collage using printed paper/illustrations from magazines.	Designing and making books for personal dictionaries.	Alphabet or dictionary of composers/musical instruments.
RHYMES AND HOMOPHONES	Collecting and presenting data, eg. frequency of letters in words; consonants/vowels.	Exploring senses (especially hearing and the ability to discriminate between sounds).	Poems from other countries. Using maps to locate countries.	Presenting rhymes/poems; borders, calligraphy, illuminated manuscripts.	Making class joke books; designing them to suit content.	Composing music to accompany rhymes. Singing poems set to music; folk songs. Selecting and combining sounds to make musical structures.
WORD FAMILIES	Roman numerals. Numerals from a variety of languages (Chinese).	Roots of scientific vocabulary. Latin plant names and parts of growing things.	Roman/Greek languages and writing. History of English language. Influences from other countries; invasions/settlers/exploration (Roman, Anglo-Saxon, Viking). Maps to locate sources of words in English; other languages encountered.	Printing; monoprints, linoprints, etc. Work of artists in the past – artefacts, architecture, sculpture.	Investigating printing presses. Designing and making printing blocks.	Instruments of the orchestra (families – strings, woodwind, brass, percussion). Music from other cultures reflecting time and place.
CURIOSITIES	Pattern and shape; different cultural traditions.	Figures in history of science (eg. Newton, Darwin). Change and growth over time (plants, animals, decay).	History of printing: monks/manuscripts – Caxton. History of English: (OE, ME). Links with religion (Chaucer and Canterbury pilgrims).	Art from different times (Celtic, Modern). Designing advertisements: images which play with words.	Designing and making board games and containers.	Musical terminology: words from Italian.